Politics for the People prov
that will be invaluable to reader:
I found it to be interesting, in:
for my own knowledge as v
on the U.S. politi

MORTON COLEMAN
Director, Institute of Politics
University of Pittsburgh

This book might well be subtitled "What Every Serious
Citizen Needs to Know About Politics." It is a readable and
informative summary of how to be effective in the
political process.

JOHN C. GREEN
Director, Ray C. Bliss Institute of Applied Politics
University of Akron

Never before has it been more important for people
of faith and other grassroots citizens to make their views
known in the political process. Bruce Barron's witty
and insightful *Politics for the People* provides
the perfect roadmap.

RALPH REED
Executive Director
Christian Coalition

Practical, readable, straightforward—a helpful
how-to manual for political engagement, written by a
practitioner immersed in politics.

RONALD J. SIDER
President
Evangelicals for Social Action

Bruce Barron has provided more than a primer
for effective political involvement by the average American
citizen who has neither large amounts of money
nor prior government contacts. He offers a pragmatic
approach to citizen activism, informed but not jaded
by his four years as a congressional staffer.

ANSON SHUPE
Professor of Sociology and Anthropology
Indiana University-Purdue University

This highly informative book is unique because it provides
an insider's view of the American political process. It is
one of the few books that actually explain the nuts and bolts
of politics. This is an important and long overdue book
for anyone who wants to become more prudent,
savvy and effective in politics.

MICHAEL CROMARTIE
Senior Fellow
Ethics and Public Policy Center

POLITICS
for the
PEOPLE

Bruce Barron

InterVarsity Press
Downers Grove, Illinois

InterVarsity Press® is the book-publishing division of InterVarsity Christian Fellowship®, a student movement active on campus at hundreds of universities, colleges and schools of nursing in the United States of America, and a member movement of the International Fellowship of Evangelical Students. For information about local and regional activities, write Public Relations Dept., InterVarsity Christian Fellowship, 6400 Schroeder Rd., P.O. Box 7895, Madison, WI 53707-7895.

Scripture quotations are from the New Revised Standard Version of the Bible, copyright 1989 by the Division of Christian Education of the National Council of the Churches of Christ in the USA. Used by permission. All rights reserved.

Cover photographs: Capitol building: Wes Thompson/The Stock Market; group of people: Phil Cantor/ SuperStock
ISBN 0-8308-1984-3

Printed in the United States of America ♾

Library of Congress Cataloging-in-Publication Data

Barron, Bruce.
    Politics for the people/Bruce Barron.
        p.   cm.
    Includes bibliographical references.
    ISBN 0-8308-1984-3 (pbk.: alk. paper)
    1. Political participation—United States.   2. Political culture—
United States.   3. United States—Politics and government.
    4. Christians—United States—Political activity.   I. Title.
JK1764.B37   1996
323'.042'0973—dc20   95-50978
                                                  CIP

18	17	16	15	14	13	12	11	10	9	8	7	6	5	4	3	2	1
11	10	09	08	07	06	05	04	03	02	01	00	99	98	97	96		

1

WANTED: HONEST POLITICIANS

. . . . . .

*O*ne week before my twenty-eighth birthday, I went to the polls and voted in an election—for the first time. I had been eligible to vote for almost ten years without ever voting. So perhaps I have more appreciation than do most politically active persons for the average citizen who says, "Keeping up with issues, programs and candidates closely enough to be able to vote intelligently just isn't worth the time!"

There are plenty of excuses:

"It's too hard to get accurate information."

"My vote won't change anything. As just one person in a nation of 260 million people, I can't have any real impact."

"Who's in office, especially at the local level, makes no difference in my life anyhow."

"Most politicians are crooked—or, at the very least, so many are crooked that I can never have confidence in any of them."

I can't promise you that by the end of this book you'll be raring to enter politics. Nor is that my goal. But I think I can make all those obstacles to meaningful participation seem less imposing to you than they may appear now. And I believe that, by the time you finish this book, you will have a better understanding of how politics works and will feel more prepared to get involved honestly and effectively at any level—from communicating with your legislators to running a campaign—should you choose to do so.

Before I appeal to your personal interests, though, let me speak briefly to your sense of patriotism and argue that it is in our country's best interest for you to be involved. You see, the survival of our great American democratic experiment depends, more than you may realize it, on the survival of the perception that *the people still have a voice in their nation's affairs.*

Take our system of collecting taxes, for example. The Internal Revenue Service may look like a mammoth bureaucracy and may sometimes feel like Big Brother, but it's not omnipresent enough to catch you if you charge some nonexistent expenses against your self-employment income or inflate your charitable contributions. The IRS's limited capacity to audit personal income-tax returns means that your chances of getting caught are minuscule. Despite this invitation to cheat the government, most Americans are pretty honest about their tax returns because they know it's the right thing to do.

But what if Americans, on a mass scale, became disgusted with their government? I think you would see the compliance rate plunge dramatically. Instead of grudgingly coming up with the money at tax time, people would actively seek ways to avoid doing so, illegally if necessary. No longer able to raise money effectively, the government would either fall apart or turn to massive use of force to compel obedience. Either anarchy or total-

8

itarianism would become a real part of our daily lives, just as it is for the people of many Latin American and African countries where the government has never attained legitimacy in the public's eyes.

Yes, the American experiment stands on shakier ground than we think. Erosion of the public trust could bring the whole system down in shambles from within just as surely as an armed takeover from abroad.

But, you say, isn't the public trust already lacking? Look at the polls that show our presidents often below a 50 percent approval rating and a great majority of Americans holding Congress in low esteem. What clearer signs of distrust do we need?

Well, that's not the same thing. To prove it, ask these disenchanted folks whether they would want to exchange the American system of government for that of any other nation. You'll find few persons ready to make the trade. Americans are not dissatisfied with their government, just with some of the people who run it. And they remain hopeful that the things they don't like can be changed and the leaders they don't like can be replaced through the democratic process.

Your involvement—or at least your sense that you could have some say in our government if you wanted to—*does* make a difference.

If I Can Do It, So Can You

I am living proof that it doesn't take half a lifetime of scheming either to become politically competent or to gain some modest degree of influence. I fell into this work rather unexpectedly, in fact. While researching a graduate dissertation, I developed a view of government that placed me closer to the core of the Republican than the Democratic party, and it occurred to me that I might be able to make some sort of civic contribution, as well as some new friendships, by volunteering with the local Republican organization. (Let me hasten to stress that I do not claim all good people are Republicans. Although my philosophy of government guided me to the Republican party, I know there are plenty of first-rate public servants in the Democratic party and plenty of disreputable persons in my own.)

A friend put me in touch with my county's Republican party chairman, and he in turn suggested that I contact a young man named Rick Santorum who had just declared his candidacy for Congress in suburban Pittsburgh. I offered the Santorum campaign my skills, which included editorial and media experience as well as solid word-processing abilities. I expected to get some typing or data-entry assignments, but within three weeks I had become the volunteer press secretary for a congressional campaign. I quickly learned that there is plenty of room in politics for people who offer their time and energy (especially to long-shot candidates) if they don't charge a fee.

Between a candidate who could think fast and a press secretary who could type fast, we produced over fifty press statements in the next nine months. A national Republican staffer called ours the most aggressive press effort in the country that year. Since most of the local media rated our chances of knocking off a seven-term incumbent as dim, I had the honor of setting records for most press releases unprinted and most press conferences unattended. But our diligence paid off in a flurry of publicity during the last few weeks, and when it was all over Rick Santorum had won 51 percent of the vote. And I had a new job on my hands, quite different from the academic career for which I had been preparing.

The campaign manager promptly invited me to move to Washington and become the congressman's official press secretary, but I had no interest in assuming the hectic life of a full-time press aide. Instead I accepted a position in Congressman Santorum's district office, where for the next four years (1991-1994) I helped solve constituents' problems, worked on district projects and tried to keep my congressman's popularity high at home.

Along the way it became increasingly apparent that I had stumbled onto something big. Doing press work for a campaign that made political history in Pittsburgh was heady in itself. But after moving onto the congressional staff, I was along for the ride as Rick Santorum made national headlines by leading the drive to expose the House Bank scandal in 1992. He then, through a new committee assignment, became the primary House Republican spokesman on welfare reform in 1993, and in 1994 he unseated another incumbent to become the youngest member of the U.S. Senate.

Over these four years, correspondence or statements I drafted for Congressman Santorum showed up in the news on several occasions ("Guess who wrote that line?" I would chuckle to my wife as she read the paper). I helped to prepare one national radio address as well as a number of Santorum's legislative proposals and speeches.

Had I moved to Washington I would have had many more such opportunities. But I was always drawn more to local projects and serving the public than to the power-charged atmosphere of Capitol Hill. The diverse activity of a congressional district office, previously unfamiliar to me, proved so captivating that when my wife was planning a trip for my birthday I suggested that she schedule a visit to another office so that we could learn how they did things.

In five years of assisting Rick Santorum's progress from political anonymity to national prominence, I had ample opportunity to observe both clean and dirty politics. I would like to think that I learned from him how to avoid dirty politics and still be successful. While I can't say we were flawless, I feel certain that we were much cleaner than most political operations of that scale. Santorum always remembered that there are higher goals in life than the next election, and he surrounded himself with people who felt the same way. Contrary to the common perception that politicians must bow to the winds of popular opinion in order to succeed, I believe Santorum succeeded in part because he gave such honest, forthright answers that people came to feel they could trust him even when they disagreed with him.

Not that our youthful good-government attitudes didn't run into reality at times. During his first campaign, Santorum had charged the incumbent with using his free mailing privileges for political gain by sending out postcards announcing his town meetings and district-wide newsletters selectively promoting his activities. Upon taking office, Santorum declared that he would make his whole voting record—not just a list of the votes he knew to be popular—available upon request, eliminate photos from his informational newsletters, and send no mass mailings to announce his town meetings. The first two commitments stuck, but the last one proved unworkable. It survived only a handful of poorly publicized meetings, capped by the one that absolutely *no one* attended—with the exception of a journalist who reported the event, complete with a photo of the miffed congressman sitting in an empty room. By the end of the first year we were sending mass mailings before our town meetings.

Many of the stories I brought home to the dinner table reinforced my wife's summary statement about politics: "It's all a game." Indeed it can feel like a game, one in which winning often depends more on deal-making and ego-stroking than on intelligent argument or good work. But while I've occasionally been discouraged at those instances where evil prevails, deceit is rewarded or money buys electoral victory, I have also come to appreciate the ways in which our system *does* respond to public input and, thereby, reflects and represents our citizens' genuine needs. Besides, even if the game is not always clean or enjoyable, it's a very important game, because the results powerfully impact how all of us live. For this reason, just as it is in our nation's interest to keep as many of us as possible engaged in the process, so it is in each individual's interest to know how to play.

I have written this book primarily to help you learn the rules of the game—how you can make your government work for you and how to influence the political process. It's not hard, but I find that most people have serious misconceptions about how to play. I certainly had quite a few. I thought elections were decided mainly by those who made better arguments on the issues; I assumed anyone who started campaigning for an office two years before the election was a self-centered victim of unbridled ambition; and it never occurred to me that people whose government benefits were getting lost in the bureaucracy should call on their legislator's district office to solve the problem. Supervising interns in a congressman's office for four years has convinced me that most undergraduate political-science majors have more misconceptions than I had—to say nothing of the general public. But when I started teaching average citizens about political involvement, I couldn't find a book that contained the information I thought people needed to know.

I hope this book will fill that gap. To keep it interesting, I have tried to illustrate my points throughout with anecdotes from real-life politics, drawing mostly on my personal experience. I have consulted with various players and observers of the game of politics to make sure that my perspective accurately reflects the real world of American politics at all levels and in all places, rather than just my own experience with a particular member of Congress in a specific geographic area. I have not, however, attempted to encompass forms of government beyond the United States. Although many of the principles I discuss are transferable to other countries and their political systems, even nearby Canada differs significantly with regard to how political parties function and

13

how citizens relate to their government.

Politician Doesn't Have to Be a Dirty Word

When I said I wanted to write a book on honest politics, some friends retorted that it would be a very short book. For most readers the word *politician* carries a negative connotation, conjuring up images of smooth-talking deceivers who make sleazy deals in secret and then market their programs to the public as wonderful reforms. Without denying that some politicians fit that image, I would like to rehabilitate the word, at least for the length of this book.

When people ask me how I can stand working in such a dirty field as politics, one of my pat answers is "There's just as much politics on a church board as there is on Capitol Hill." I have found that this answer has silenced every questioner who has ever served on a church board. No, I'm not claiming that church boards are notoriously dishonest or that they function exactly like civil governments. But the questioner immediately recognizes that church committees present most of the same dynamics as legislative bodies: misunderstanding, contentiousness, heated rhetoric, compromise, the need to deal diplomatically with varied personalities.

Politics is simply the art of governing the *polis* (Greek for "city") or county or state or nation. It is inherently volatile and unpredictable, since it involves dealing with persons, but it is not inherently dirty. The risk of corruption may be greater at your state capitol than in your local church, because of the greater amount of money and power at stake, but the interpersonal processes are essentially similar. So when you see the word *politician* in this book, please think of it simply as a noun that describes someone who engages in politics, not as an ugly label. Or at the very least, if you can't eliminate your negative reaction to the word, keep in mind that this author has a soft spot for politicians because he is one.

14

You Might Even Enjoy It

Having already presented patriotic and utilitarian reasons for getting involved in politics, let me add that political participation can be deeply rewarding, even downright fun. Becoming involved in your government offers chances to help your neighbors in concrete ways. The intensity of a campaign builds lasting friendships; you also get a lot of free pizza, and, if your candidate posts an upset win, your memories of election-night euphoria will last a lifetime. Volunteering for a political party or your town's planning commission gives you the opportunity to meet people who share your interests. If you like dealing with the public, you'll love many of the regular activities of local politics.

In addition, how your government operates can have a considerable direct impact on your life. People who say they don't care who runs their community suddenly change their tune if their taxes soar or if they are denied a building permit. You may not think it matters who your member of Congress is, but if your child wants to go to college at the Air Force Academy and you discover that your member of Congress dispenses the military academy appointments in your city as political favors, your indifference will not last long. On a more mundane level, if you ever run into a seemingly unsolvable personal problem with the government, you will deeply appreciate any clout your local representative can exercise to resolve it.

To emphasize the relevance of government to your everyday life, I will address in chapter two how you can get your government to work for you. This priority reverses most politicians' tendency to treat lawmaking as their important activity and serving constituents as secondary—an understandable bias, since elected officials do much of the lawmaking themselves while their staffs do the constituent service, but nevertheless one that should be counterbalanced. Starting with this topic also lets me spin, before I can put any readers to sleep, a few of my favorite tales

15

from my own experience as a congressional aide. Along with the humor, however, I also seek to offer useful insight into some of the more valuable though less noticed aspects of our government process.

Chapter three turns to the legislative side of our political system, examining how you can influence your legislators. If you fail to influence them you will probably want to replace them, so chapter four takes the next logical step by discussing how you can get involved effectively in campaigns and elections.

The next three chapters address some of the questions I have most often been asked in my efforts to do and to teach honest politics. Chapter five looks at the temptations that push many politicians to engage in unprincipled or dishonest activity—and at how an honest public servant can avert those pitfalls without sabotaging his or her political career. Next, since the main way to become politically active is through one of the two major political parties, chapter six discusses the role of the parties and whether and how you should pursue involvement in a party. Chapter seven offers suggestions on how to acquire reliable, timely information so as to monitor and impact the political process as effectively as possible.

Successful political involvement results from a variety of skills and personality traits, several of which I describe in chapter eight as I portray the "physique" of a politician. I believe the single most indispensable component of that physique is thick skin, without which you should never expect either to go very far in politics or to enjoy it for very long. I also seek to identify other key talents that will make your political activity both more productive and more enjoyable.

I have reserved my comments on religion and politics for chapter nine so as to mirror my beliefs as to how religion and politics should mix. I am an active Christian who entered politics desiring to rehabilitate in some small way, through honest and

16

compassionate public service, the often shoddy image of Christians in government. One of my essential operating principles, and one I believe all Christians would do well to adopt, is that people of faith should not advocate as public policy any views they cannot defend on public (as opposed to explicitly religious) grounds. In other words, if you can't justify a policy apart from your religion, you have no basis for requiring nonbelievers to obey it.

In that spirit I will restrain myself from preaching between this paragraph and chapter nine. Not that I consider Christianity irrelevant to doing honest politics; on the contrary, I believe Christian truth often illuminates good politics more clearly, especially in the crucial areas of integrity and public servanthood. But in chapters two through eight I have tried to keep the discussion relevant to *all* readers by omitting the explicitly Christian arguments and illustrations I might use when teaching in a church setting. Even in chapter nine, where my discussion of the proper relationship between religion and politics may move a bit further from exposition into advocacy, I have tried to make the presentation instructive and applicable to persons of both religious and nonreligious persuasions. If I have remained true to my own operating principles, you should find this book relevant to your life situation whether or not you share my theological convictions.

You should not expect that this book will equip you to win all the political battles you choose to enter. On the contrary, an effective politician must be prepared to lose sometimes. Not even in the best of democracies does right or wisdom always prevail, and our democratic system constantly compels compromise with competing influences. But whatever you do, if you do it with honesty and sincerity, will benefit all of us more than if you hadn't bothered to try, and you can never know how much impact you might be able to achieve until you do try.

17

At the very least, I hope to convince you that political power is not reserved for insiders, lobbyists and millionaires—and that you too have the potential to make a difference wherever you start.

2

MAKING
GOVERNMENT
WORK FOR YOU

. . . .

O n January 3, 1991, Rick Santorum took the oath of office as a freshman member of the U.S. House of Representatives. While Pittsburgh-area media highlighted his swearing-in ceremony on Capitol Hill, his district office (and my career in government) opened with considerably less fanfare. Had you wanted to call and welcome us to our new office, you couldn't have done so: we had no phones. The eight weeks since election day had not been quite enough time to prepare a full-service operation.

By week's end we had phones (though computers took another month), in time for the deluge of callers seeking to influence Congressman Santorum's momentous first vote—on whether to authorize the use of American military force to liberate Kuwait. We could have picked a better time to get started. Our politically uninitiated district staff gamely tried to communicate the congressman's stated position consistently, but callers didn't always get the same message, and soon local talk shows were reporting embarrassingly conflicting reports of where he stood.

That episode quickly taught us why politicians choose their words so cautiously; you would too if you knew any ill-advised words would show up on that evening's news. But even amidst the historic debate that preceded the brief Persian Gulf War, other discoveries captured my interest more than did the involvement with national issues.

I had long known that people could call their legislator's district office to advise him or her how to vote, but I never knew that you could also call that same office to get birthday greetings (for persons age eighty or over) or anniversary cards (for couples married at least fifty years) from the White House. Nor did I know that by calling your member of Congress you can get free tickets for special White House tours or obtain an American flag that has flown over the U.S. Capitol. (I have yet to discern how that momentary unfurling over the Capitol makes a flag superior, but those are hot items in congressional offices.)

Then came the calls for personal assistance with the federal government. One constituent had failed, despite repeated correspondence with the Internal Revenue Service, to resolve an erroneous tax levy. Another claimed to have been dismissed improperly from his federal job. Another wanted reconsideration of a medical bill Medicare had refused to reimburse. Others sought federal employment. One unforgettable inquirer insisted that the congressman personally direct the U.S. Postal Service to bring his mail to his porch rather than leave it in a curbside mailbox.

With help from a more experienced congressional office nearby, we quickly developed procedures for managing this constituent casework. We learned that every day we would be signing the congressman's name to letters he would never read. We also learned how effective these inquiries could be. The IRS, for example, gave us a phone number that directly accessed its Pittsburgh regional director's office, as well as the assurance that any written inquiries from the office of a member of Congress ("congressionals," for short) would receive top priority.

It never would have occurred to me, if I had a problem with the IRS or any other federal agency, to contact my congressman's office. But I found that by carrying the clout of a congressman I could cut through red tape, not only at government agencies but even at private companies that did not want to risk offending a prominent politician. We applied our influence effectively in such a wide variety of areas—sometimes, admittedly, only as a reluctant concession to unrelenting constituents—that when my wife lamented that our next-door neighbor had painted her house an unattractive color, I suggested that perhaps we could call our congressman.

That misfortune probably fell outside any public official's jurisdiction, but just learning the dozens of federal agencies over which we did have jurisdiction and how to deal with them offered me an intellectual challenge as great as my Ph.D. studies. In a typical day I might help a business entrepreneur find loan assistance, question environmental agencies about the safety of a proposed incinerator, track down the Americans with Disabilities Act regulations for the height of pay phones, analyze residents' complaints about a federally funded road reconstruction, and join my boss on a visit to a model elementary-school program.

The job brought emotional as well as intellectual challenges. Along with the man who vowed to knock the congressman out of office because we couldn't get his mailbox moved to his doorstep, I remember the exotic dancer who wanted government aid to avert foreclosure on her home but was unable to document her sources of income. Several persons sought our protection from messages they believed the Federal Communications Commission was sending through their radios. A self-employed marketing specialist sought public support for his grandiose plan to cement world peace by transforming the United Nations into the Forever United Nations (FUN), complete with FUN international tours, FUN Olympics, FUN credit cards, and so on. Each time a politician graciously answered his inquiry with "Your idea is fascinating, but unfortunately it lies beyond my jurisdiction to implement," he interpreted the letter as an endorsement and added the writer's name to his growing list of supposed backers. Along with these memorable constituents came a collection of individuals who phoned regularly to sound off on the issue of the day, thereby qualifying for what we euphemistically called our "frequent caller list" of persons with whom we should not spend too much time.

Working for a congressman offered more than strenuous intellectual exercise and some heart-rending stories, however. Most of all, it was a chance to see the government process help people. Bombarded by stories of waste, fraud, bureaucratic inefficiency, partisanship and dishonesty, we forget that sometimes our system of government *actually works*. Just as I had no clue as to how an elected official's local office can help people until I worked in one, I'm sure many readers would benefit from learning too. Let's talk first about *how* you can make use of your local offices; then we'll look at *why* they work as they do.

Government on Call

You should contact your legislators for personal help when you believe a government agency has not treated you fairly or when you need something in a hurry. Don't wear out your welcome by calling when it's not necessary or when the bureaucracy is handling your paperwork just fine. But if your driver's license is stolen and you need a replacement immediately, a visit to your state representative's office should produce better results than half a dozen calls to the Department of Motor Vehicles.

When you call, ask for the staff member who handles the area of concern to you—not for the legislator personally, who is seldom involved with such matters. Rather than telling your whole story on the phone (unless it's an emergency), explain what you are seeking and ask if it is appropriate to write the legislator a letter requesting assistance in that matter. The office will need formal written authorization before it can request disclosure of your personal records, and in any case a written summary both increases your credibility and helps the staff member grasp the facts of the case quickly and accurately. Whether verbally or in writing, your job is to provide as succinct and organized a summary as possible of what has taken place, to indicate whom you have already contacted in trying to solve the problem, and to specify what action you want the legislator's office to take or what questions you want answered.

Once the office has assembled the information it needs, it will contact the agency involved—at a higher level than you can access directly. A written request from a legislator's office compels a written, formal reply, usually within three weeks. (Since staff often have heavy caseloads, you should take it as your responsibility to remind the aide to follow up if a timely reply is not received.) The legislator's inquiry will most likely generate more careful review of your case by a supervisor. Even if the letter is referred to the same agency bureaucrat with whom you were dealing in the first place, that bureaucrat is now facing the likelihood of increased scrutiny from his or her boss and from an elected official. This added attention, combined with your representative's vested interest in satisfying you, will generally ensure you the most favorable treatment to which you are entitled. Legislators cannot order an agency to give you more benefits than the law requires, but at the very least they can secure and interpret for you a complete explanation of the relevant statutes or regulations governing your situation.

In four years of constituent service I cannot recall a single person who regretted having contacted the legislator's office with a casework problem; I can, however, remember many who wished they had come to us sooner. A woman who was ruining both her emotional equilibrium and her long-distance phone budget over a student loan billing error got a written guarantee from the Department of Education that she could ignore the bills their contractor's computer continued to send her. (Always get such assurances in writing, as your legal protection in case of further difficulties.) A family solved its saga of basement floods because I delivered their information to the transportation department's regional director and asked him to investigate the drainage off the roadway. We couldn't bump people up the waiting list for publicly funded services (happily, our bureaucracy seldom descends to the brazen political favoritism associated with many bribe-ridden countries of the world). But in cases entailing more subjective judgment, such as how much federally funded job-retraining assistance a laid-off worker could receive, our inquiries frequently appeared to benefit the constituent.

Even where the result is unchanged, the constituent often receives information he or she could not otherwise have secured without retaining a lawyer. Legislators' aides (good ones, at least) understand government processes well enough to cut through delays, assess the likelihood of a favorable ruling, and interpret the situation helpfully for frustrated citizens—all without charge. In a case that hinges on disputed facts or interpretations of law, the constituent may still need to pursue the matter in court. But as I often pointed out to constituents, "You've already paid for me with your tax dollars, so you should get as much help out of me as you can before you start paying a lawyer."

Finally, this exchange with the elected legislator's office affords constituents who discover that the perceived injustice they have experienced is legal an opportunity to suggest a change in the law. I observed many occasions where one or two constituent complaints initiated the process by which my own congressman became an advocate for the change those constituents sought. Even at the local level, a lone voice will not achieve any major change, but it may reinforce what other "lone voices" have been saying elsewhere, or it may heighten awareness of the issue and thus awaken other voices on your behalf. Change seldom happens fast, but every change has to begin somewhere, and it might as well begin with you.

It Sure Beats Depending on an Unelected Bureaucrat

When I began handling casework for a legislative office, I felt the process seemed inefficient, if not ridiculous. People who had problems with the government would tell me their problem, I would tell the agency, the agency would research the matter and respond to our office, and I would relay the answer to the constituent. Why, I wondered, should we require a minimum of four exchanges of information among at least three parties just to provide citizens with answers they should have been able to get directly?

In the ideal world, we wouldn't. But in the real world, especially in the case of an organization as enormous as the U.S. government, ignorance, misunderstanding and errors abound, and federal employees are not always attentive and responsive. If you've ever tried to get a frazzled Social Security Administration staffer to put aside that depressing case backlog and pile of unreturned messages and spend an extra hour helping you understand the system, you know what I mean.

The answer—unless we want a system in which any of us could at any time become a defenseless victim of our own government—is to give every citizen access to at least one person whose job description includes making the government user-friendly and who is personally accountable to that citizen. Our system gives you such a person. In fact, it gives you five at the federal level alone, but the president and vice president are hard to reach, and in populous states your two U.S. senators aren't much closer. No matter where you live, however, your member of Congress and his or her staff should be more accessible, because their job security is more likely to depend on their ability to keep people like you happy.

If you have always thought a legislator's job entailed simply voting on issues and obtaining money for programs in his or her district, think again. I believe that making the government user-friendly for constituents is one of the most important roles an elected official can play. Thus I consider it part of the genius of our democratic republic, not an unavoidable misfortune, that politicians' reelection chances can be affected by how well their office handles casework.

Although I like to think of myself as a deeply compassionate person, I know that my energetic commitment to serving constituents derived partly from my keen awareness of the potential political impact of my service. Unlike the unseen, unappreciated (and, as a result, often unmotivated) welfare caseworker, I carried out assignments that voters would associate with their congressman and which could, consequently, win or lose the next election (and decide whether I would still have a job). I realized the power of that motivation most fully in 1992, when Rick Santorum's congressional district was substantially redrawn, as is required every ten years following each census, so that we were campaigning for reelection in a district 60 percent of which was new territory. I did my best to handle every request professionally that year, but calls from the new district grabbed my attention far more easily, while (particularly as the election neared) inquiries from the old district felt like unwanted distractions.

26

As we will observe repeatedly in this book, your influence in dealing with your representatives is directly related to your ability to defeat them at the polls if you so choose. This is why we all should prefer competitive elections rather than uncontested incumbents: politicians who no longer fear the voters will tend not to listen to them as carefully. Perhaps the only thing worse than an electorally safe politician, from the constituent's perspective, is the one who has announced his retirement; he and his staff are probably working less than ever, and perhaps getting paid more than ever while collecting bonuses from the Member's accumulated, nontransferable payroll funds. An intern I was supervising once remarked that, while I ran her ragged in our strenuous desire to satisfy every constituent, her boyfriend, interning for an outgoing congressman, was spending the day on the golf course with his boss!

(By the way, the dynamics of constituent casework are one reason why I am at best lukewarm about proposals to limit the terms elected officials may serve. Politicians consumed with their career advancement are bad, but politicians who do not see serving their constituency as a means to career advancement may be worse.)

I can't say I endorse all the ways our system gives incumbents opportunities to do favors that enhance their reelection prospects. I don't think your member of Congress should be, at the federal level, the route by which to obtain special White House tour tickets or presidential greeting cards. In an even more galling example, my home state of Pennsylvania has long granted each legislator a personal pot of public money, known as "Legislative Initiative Grants," to dispense to nonprofit or municipal needs as he or she sees fit (endearing himself to those organizations and reaping undeserved positive media attention while doing so). These questionable uses of public resources result because the rules governing the activity of legislative offices are set by the legislators themselves, who are unlikely to support reforms that endanger their own job security. With the fox guarding the chicken coop, only a massive public outcry will stop these or other practices (such as generous mailing privileges, large staffs, and campaign finance laws) that favor incumbents.

While working as a congressional aide I became convinced that staff allotments could be cut by 25 percent with minimal impact on the offices' ability to perform their essential duties. Such a cut would prevent congressional offices from doing only those tasks that are politically beneficial, or demanded by constituents unwilling to help themselves, but unnecessary. I also, however, reject the opposite extreme—namely, the contention by some policy wonks that the purpose of legislators is to legislate and that they should be judged on their legislative record, not their constituent service. As government's role in our society has greatly expanded in recent decades (a development I regret, but a fact of contemporary America nevertheless), government becomes, for many citizens, more a source of assistance than a maker and enforcer of laws. For these persons a legislator's value lies in his or her ability to serve them, not his or her policy stances. It is perfectly appropriate for them to use this criterion in deciding for whom they will vote.

In cases of substantive need, whether it be interpreting legislation or unraveling a government agency's error, the current system helps everyone. It motivates politicians to earn their constituents' approval by solving real problems and judges them by their capacity to do so. Though the squeakiest or the most influential wheel may sometimes get the grease, that is better than a system in which people with problems cannot squeak at all. Americans should not take for granted how easily we can get someone to hear and respond to us when we squeak.

The same rules of constituent service apply, often with a more discernible personal touch, at the most local levels of government, where little-noticed officials jump at the chance to earn favor. Thus, if you have a problem with snow removal or garbage pick-up, don't just call your town's public works department; phone your mayor or council member too and ask them to make sure your concern is resolved promptly. Or, if you have a good idea for your elementary school, call your school board members as well as your principal. You might be surprised—provided that you are reasonable, respectful, and not too pushy—at how much attention you get.

More Offbeat Ideas

Beyond all this, you can often get even more unexpected treasures from your representatives if you know how to ask. Just don't tell the staff member, who may feel trapped between an inward desire to turn you down and an overpowering fear of offending a constituent, that you got these ideas from me.

Freebies. If you're planning to visit Washington, D.C., or your state capitol, your legislator's office probably has more helpful information than the Automobile Club. Your member of Congress can get you special tickets to many of Washington's leading attractions if you ask far enough in advance. The Congressional Research Service publishes thorough, informative summary papers on every public-policy issue of current interest; you can't call CRS yourself, but your senator or representative can order what you want and pass it on to you for no charge. (I wish I had known about CRS when writing my high-school research papers.) The list of free publications available from county, state and federal departments is virtually endless.

Help with community activities. You don't have to limit your requests to matters within your legislators' formal jurisdiction. As a congressional aide I was drawn (along with my expertise, follow-up research, and my boss's clout) into many local matters by constituents who said, "It's not a federal issue, but we know the congressman cares about . . ." Most aides will recognize that, in matters of community-wide significance, it's better to get involved in any way possible than to decline and leave the impression that the Member didn't want to help. Even on private-sector matters like a grant application to a foundation or land negotiations with a prominent local corporation, the representative's intervention increases your credibility and brings one valuable commodity you may not possess on your own: the ability to get your calls returned.

The congressional staff on which I worked helped to build a playground, refurbish a Habitat for Humanity house and clear a hiking trail, all as staff projects in our free time but at the Member's direction. Don't expect your local office to say yes to all such requests. But don't hesitate to ask—the worst they can say is no.

Networking. Besides, you never know what friendships your representative may be able to call on. An elected official deals with people from every sector of society, most of whom have a personal interest in gaining their legislator's favor and many of whom, because they like the Member, will do something to help him or her look good. As a result, a call to the legislator's office might get you unexpected help. During my tenure as an aide I helped constituents get free accounting advice, job interviews (though we never asked a public agency or private company to give anyone a job, only a fair shot at one) and free dirt for Little League baseball diamonds, just to name a few unusual benefits. Moreover, our exposure to almost everything going on in our communities gave us an encyclopedic capacity to link callers with the agencies, officials, peers or experts best able to help address their need. Seldom were we not able at least to lead constituents, whatever their concern, to someone who could help them better than we could and whom they may not have found on their own.

Petty cash. If you don't consider it blackmail, you can sometimes get a little money for your favorite community project. Candidates for local office will contribute $25 to your cause rather than risk the political fallout of not giving—provided that the decision whether to give will be widely known, such as by an ad or lack thereof in a banquet program. Your Little League team or Scout troop can bring in a few hundred dollars, in years with several contested races, by inviting each candidate for state, county or municipal office to give a small contribution.

Be sure to explain, with your request, how the candidate's donation will be announced publicly and how many persons will see or hear the announcement. If the candidate's opponent has already given, you can diplomatically mention this, but don't threaten retribution against anyone who does not instantly agree to give. Most politicians recognize the necessity of these donations, even if they have no personal enthusiasm for your cause, and you don't want to leave them with an unpleasant memory of this solicitation. To those who argue that this approach feeds egotistical politicians' interest in self-promotion or misuses their office, I respond that elections inevitably entail self-promotion and that the candidates should have known what they were getting into before they started. But if you're still uncomfortable with asking for these contributions, feel free to abstain and leave more money in the pot for my group.

Who Does All the Work Anyhow?

Some of the most humorous calls I experienced as a congressional aide came from persons who eagerly asked, "Is the congressman in?" and then, when persuaded to share their concern with a staff member, went on to describe a mundane, garden-variety piece of federal agency casework. I would be tempted to wonder whether these people really think their congressman spends his time resolving individual Social Security or Veterans Administration cases, had I not also observed the many people who approached my boss after one of his town meetings to say, with the deepest gratitude and sincerity in their voice, "Thank you so much for getting my son his military pension."

On such occasions the elected official, if he or she has any tact, accepts the compliment with grace, declining to admit that he himself never saw the case. One senses that such persons want to believe they have personal access to their legislators when they need it, just as supporters of television evangelists want to believe their beloved preacher personally agonizes over the prayer requests they send with their contributions. It is kinder and wiser to leave that perception intact than to try to educate these persons as to how a legislative office operates. (Accordingly, I hope none of them stumble upon this book.)

Legislative offices tend to perpetuate the perception of the Member's personal involvement, because it helps to perpetuate the Member's career. Aides are taught, if they resolve a constituent inquiry favorably by phone, to send a follow-up letter over the legislator's signature, stating, "I am pleased that my office was able to assist you, . . ." with the goal of engraving a positive image of that official in the recipient's mind. My office reduced the need for forgery somewhat when it acquired the capacity to produce a laser-printed facsimile of the congressman's signature on outgoing mail. Nevertheless, interns regularly expressed surprise at the amount of activity our office carried out—not just daily casework but community involvement, grant support letters, and high-level policy inquiries—without informing the boss until the next monthly report, if at all.

At the upper levels of government, that's the only way an effective office can operate. I once visited another congressional office which seemed to operate smoothly except for one quirk: the Member (who represented a politically secure, largely rural district) had instructed staff to reserve all outgoing mail for his personal review and signature. When I returned home and described my visit, a coworker aptly commented, "There's a congressman who must have nothing better to do." Most legislators are consumed with more pressing matters that they alone can handle, and so they must trust their staff to carry out the office's regular functions. The more work the Member and top aides can trust the rest of the staff to perform properly without direct supervision, the more gets done.

This is why hiring a staff is one of the most significant decisions a legislator makes: the staff, once selected, will play a major role in making or breaking the boss's own future. At the same time, however, it remains appropriate to describe all the office's work as taking place in the Member's name. The Member will not personally do all the work, but he or she sets the office policy as to what work will be done, who will do it, and what actions can or cannot be taken without higher-level approval. Thus I could always, in good conscience and not just for political purposes, remind constituents who thanked me for my help—especially in those nontraditional forms of congressional service like finding dirt for a baseball field—that I could do nothing without my congressman's approval and authority.

This peek at the operation of a legislative office reminds us that honest politics entails two largely distinct spheres of activity. It includes not only the votes, funding awards, and policy statements that make the newspaper, but also the daily activity of ensuring that our government equitably serves all its citizens. The two functions are interrelated, as casework inquiries alert legislators to systemic problems that need attention; for example, the flood of complaints related to Social Security has led to the creation of the Social Security Administration as an independent agency, separate from the department in which it was formerly contained, and the establishment of procedures to reduce backlogs. But the legislative and constituent-service functions should also be separable. When you are contesting a Social Security underpayment, whether you support your legislator's policy positions should be irrelevant, both to you and to the staff member whose assistance you seek. Thus you should never be bashful about accepting your representative's help in areas of constituent service while trying to influence or even oppose that same representative in areas of policy debate. In the next chapter we will examine how you can exert that influence most fruitfully.

3

GETTING YOUR
LEGISLATOR
TO LISTEN

. . . .

A socially conservative lobbying organization was trying to round up support for its opposition to federal gay-rights legislation. "Send us $10 and we'll send a telegram to your congressman and your two senators, letting them know how you feel about this threat to our society," its advertisement proclaimed.

I was not impressed by the offer. I knew very well that concerned constituents could have more impact on their representatives by making three quick and inexpensive phone calls to the officials' district offices than by paying $10 for three impersonal form letters. More disturbing, I suspected that the organization's staff knew this too—but had felt compelled to use this device as a fundraising tactic.

Having been on the receiving end of constituent letters and

calls for four years, I know how you can maximize your influence when communicating with your elected representatives. You may also, along the way, make your legislators' aides work harder. But that's their problem, not yours.

Form Letters and Better

Let's start with the least effective forms of communication and work upward. Many organizations, usually in conjunction with a fundraising appeal, provide preformed postcards, letters or telegrams which you can sign and send to your legislators. Such mass campaigns are barely worth the paper on which they are printed. Elected officials and staff know that these form-letter operations reflect minimal effort and expense by each sender. The constituent's total investment is a signature, thirty seconds of time and twenty or thirty cents for a stamp. (And sometimes the group orchestrating this mail campaign is supplying the stamps!) Persons who devote so little effort to articulating their opinion may not even bother to notice how their legislator finally votes on the issue.

In fact, these mass-mail charades are even worse than futile, because they enable the representative to influence *you*. Your postcard, by revealing where you stand on a particular issue, enables the legislator to selectively feed you information designed to win you over.

For example, when the U.S. House of Representatives was considering legislation to limit businesses' ability to hire permanent replacements for striking workers, congressional offices received thousands of prefabricated postcards from union members supporting the bill. Staff in our office entered the names and addresses in our database with a special prolabor designation, so that when the congressman cast another prolabor vote in the future we could send them a letter. Such letters typically begin, "Knowing of your interest in issues of concern to organized labor,

36

I wanted to advise you of action I recently took on your behalf in Congress." Rest assured that when the legislator casts a vote contrary to the wishes of organized labor, these people don't receive any letter.

Modern technology, which has made such targeted constituent mailings easy to produce, gives incumbents an added advantage. So, when you hear your representative say her office has obtained an advanced computer system so as to serve her constituents better, keep in mind that she is also using taxpayer funds (legally) to help herself get reelected. Similarly, when your legislator sends you a survey "because I want to have the benefit of your views on the issues I face," he may just want to find out how to code you in his computer.

Of course, any time you communicate with the legislator, whether by form letter or in more intelligent fashion, you give the legislator a chance to code you. Therefore, you should remain aware that, once you have expressed your view on an issue, the representative may feed you selective information on that issue in the future. Armed with this knowledge, you can better concentrate on influencing rather than being influenced.

A personal phone call or, better yet, a concise, individually written letter will carry more weight than any form letter. These forms of communication show that you care enough about the issue at hand to act independently or even prepare an original statement on it. Or, if you are participating in an organized advocacy campaign, a stream of incessant phone calls will exert far more influence on an office than a pile of form letters can.

Before you make the contact, become as informed as possible (from news sources or organizations involved with the issue) regarding the proposed legislation and its status, so that you don't lobby federal representatives on a state bill or mislead a staff member with an inaccurate bill number. It is always appropriate to ask for a written reply and to follow up with a reminder call a few weeks later if the reply hasn't arrived.

Will representatives actually read your letter? At the state or federal level, probably not. The volume of mail far exceeds their reading time. But if you know the internal process, you can increase the influence your correspondence will carry.

Keep in mind that every elected official wants to answer all correspondence promptly, but also with as little effort as possible. Staff won't achieve the legislator's goals if they expend too much of their resources mired in answering mail. Therefore, offices will normally prepare a form letter that addresses each issue of current concern, in a sufficiently broad way so as to answer most inquiries on that issue. If the office has a form reply suitable to respond to your letter, the legislative correspondent will dutifully hit the right buttons on the computer, and you will receive a kind but "boilerplate" reply. If the legislator is keeping a record of constituent opinion on the issue, your views will at least enter into the tabulation; if not, your opinion will go down in history as simply a tiny portion of one staffer's daily mail quota.

If you are seeking only to learn the Member's position on that issue, the form letter will suffice. (You can show your sophistication when you call the office by stating, "Just send me your standard response on this issue; I don't want to take up any more of your time until I really need it." You can even ask for three different form letters at once without feeling you've become a burden.) But if you want your letter to carry influence, it must either catch the interest of the particular staff member who first reads it or elude the expansive reach of those one-size-fits-all form letters.

Those two options afford you two courses of action. First, you can get to know the staff member who handles that issue for the legislator. This approach is especially useful if you expect to communicate frequently on bills within a specific legislative area, such as education or agriculture. Staff members like to be noticed too. They can appreciate good ideas, and in their areas of legislative specialization they usually know more details than their boss. From a staffer you can learn where the Member stands on your issue, what types of arguments may prove persuasive, and how to present them. You also create in that staffer a sense of personal accountability to follow up on and respond to your future communications.

Alternatively, your letter can elude relegation to the form-reply department and compel more careful attention if you skillfully pose a question too specific for any form letter. For example, if you dislike your governor's proposal to reform health care in your state, don't just express your opposition and request a reply. Instead, ask your state legislator to indicate whether he or she shares your view that chiropractic care should be reimbursed, or what implications he believes his counterproposals would have on nursing homes.

Legislative staff will not thank you for requiring additional work of them (just as they already frown at me for giving people this idea), but they will also acknowledge your request as legitimate and deserving of a specially composed reply. And if the aide doesn't know how the Member would answer your specific question, that question, or perhaps even the whole letter, will be passed along for the representative's personal attention.

Should you by some chance receive an unresponsive form-letter reply, politely but firmly call back to indicate that you still want a complete answer to your initial questions and that you will provide a fresh copy of your letter if necessary in order to get that answer. If you show you are serious about getting an answer, staff will recognize that it is in their best interest to respond fully. They know that the constituents persistent and thorough enough to follow up in this way are also the ones most capable of advancing the opponent's campaign if not satisfied with the incumbent's service.

What to Ask For

To do effective advocacy you must also know what to ask for. Politicians want to satisfy you while at the same time doing as little as possible that would upset those who hold a position opposed to yours. They want to win you over while not losing any other friends in the process.

And the politicians know the system better than you. If you let them get away with it, they might write back "I can assure you that I will support your bill if it comes to the floor for a vote" while (unknown to you) pleasing the other side by making sure the bill never gets out of committee and onto the floor. Or they will tell you they support your bill while failing to tell you they also support a series of amendments that would negate the bill's impact. Or they will cite a recent vote in support of your position, without mentioning that that particular bill was a strictly commemorative measure that passed unanimously. Or they will promise general support for the program you want retained, figuring that you probably won't track what they do during the actual budgeting process anyhow.

Understanding the legislative process helps you know how to request appropriate, meaningful action from your representatives and to avoid being misled by sweet-sounding but insignificant expressions of support. The accompanying chart details the normal process by which proposed bills are considered in a state or federal legislature. Note that, in most cases, a committee with jurisdiction over the particular area of legislation (and often a subcommittee before that) must approve a bill before it comes to the floor (that is, to the full legislative body) for consideration and a final vote.

How a Bill Becomes a Law (Congressional Version)

What Congress Does	What You Do
	1. Ask your legislator to introduce legislation
2. Legislator introduces bill (in either House or Senate, except that measures governing taxation must originate in House)	
3. Bill is referred to committee(s) and subcommittee(s) which may discuss, hold hearings, amend	
	4. Ask your legislator to cosponsor/ oppose; ask legislators on the relevant committees to support/oppose
5. Committee votes to send bill to floor. Amendments may also occur on the floor.	
	6. Ask your legislator (and any others you can influence) to support/oppose/amend
7. If bill passes, same process must occur in other chamber	
8. If House and Senate pass similar but differing versions of bill, conferees are selected to work out differences	
	9. Ask conferees to include/delete items when preparing conference report
10. After differences are worked out, bill returns to House and Senate for final vote	
	11. Ask legislator to support/oppose
12. Bill passes and is sent to president	
	13. Ask president to sign/veto
14. President signs bill into law	
	15. Campaign for the reelection or replacement of your legislator or president

State legislatures generally follow the same process in considering legislation and sending it, if passed in both legislative chambers, to the governor of that state for signature. Nebraska's legislature has only one chamber.

41

Of course there are special cases and exceptions, among which the following examples of congressional procedure are worth noting:

Authorization and appropriation. Congress follows a two-step process in funding a program. First it considers the merits of the program itself and authorizes spending up to a certain amount of money on it; then it appropriates, each year, the actual amount of money that program will receive. The amount appropriated seldom equals the amount authorized. Therefore, if you want to see more bridges and highways repaired, you can't rest easy when Congress authorizes a major multiyear transportation plan; you have to come back each year and urge Congress to actually appropriate the amount authorized (known as "full funding") or as close to that figure as possible.

Discharge petitions. In the U.S. House, a bill blocked by an unsupportive committee can be "discharged" from that committee and moved directly to the full House for consideration if a majority of members (218 out of 435) sign a discharge petition. In 1993 a major rules change made the list of signers of a discharge petition public knowledge. Accordingly, no longer can your representative publicly lament that a bill is stuck in committee while privately refusing to sign the discharge petition out of deference to a committee chairperson from whom he or she wants favors.

Constitutional amendments. Congress cannot enforce a law that the courts declare to be contrary to the U.S. Constitution (for example, the Supreme Court has determined that laws prohibiting flag-burning violate the Constitution's guarantee of freedom of speech). In these cases Congress must amend the Constitution itself—a process that, so as to preclude hasty revisions in the very foundations of our government, requires more than a simple majority vote. Not only must both chambers of Congress pass a constitutional amendment by a two-thirds margin, but three-fourths of the states must also ratify it in their own legislatures.

Filibusters. In the U.S. Senate, although a majority of voting members can pass a bill, a three-fifths majority is needed to cut off debate. As a result, a unified group of forty-one senators can block passage of a bill simply by engaging in endless chatter, or "filibuster." Those wanting to pass the bill must offer additional concessions until they can get at least sixty of the one hundred senators on their side. Supporters of the filibuster rule see it as an additional checks-and-balances mechanism preventing a bare majority from rushing forward with legislation that a substantial minority of senators strongly opposes. Opponents of this rule see it as permitting a minority to play havoc with the majority and bog down the legislative process even further. In any case, this is one of many factors that cause the U.S. Senate to act more deliberately and with broader consensus than is required in the House.

As these rules illustrate, you may want to request various actions from your legislator beyond promising to vote for or against a certain bill. For instance, if a bill has recently been introduced (i.e., initially proposed and referred to a committee) or is languishing in that committee, you can ask your legislator not just to promise support but to *cosponsor* the bill. Cosponsorship indicates formal, recorded support and often makes it easier for that Member's closest colleagues to support the bill as well. State or federal legislative staff can immediately access by computer a list of current cosponsors of any pending bill, and if they see some of their boss's ideological friends on the list, they will be more likely to give the proposal serious consideration.

You can also ask your representative to make a public statement on behalf of the bill when it comes up for debate, or to send a letter to all fellow members urging their support. Your goal is to persuade your legislator to offer not just passive support but active advocacy. Whatever commitments you secure, get them in writing; a politician can deny a verbal commitment or claim amnesia, but a written commitment can be repudiated only with considerable embarrassment.

If This Is Too Complicated . . .

By this point you may be feeling that the demands of the political process exceed your amount of interest or free time. You started this book looking for simple instruction, not for an exhortation to study the rules of legislative debate. If so, that's fine. Any level of constructive involvement beats noninvolvement. But if you are going to limit your interaction to periodic phone calls demanding more prisons and lower taxes, you must also recognize that your degree of influence will generally be commensurate with the limited intensity and sophistication of your involvement.

Politics may be a game, but it is also a serious business. Most of its practitioners relish not just the pursuit of fame and power but also the complex, difficult challenge of crafting good public policy—or, if they themselves don't like doing policy, they recognize that in order to look good they must surround themselves with people who do. Accordingly, if you want your voice to carry much weight, you must equip it with weighty, well-reasoned arguments. Alternatively, you can exert raw political muscle rather than persuasion, but only if you can position yourself as the spokesperson for many more voters than just yourself, as discussed later in this chapter. Either way, although a little effort may carry you farther than you anticipated, don't expect that lack of effort will carry you anywhere.

Getting the Legislator to Budge

Even if you do write your representative a good letter, can it really have much influence? That depends on several factors, the first of which is the legislator's prior commitments on the issue.

Abortion activists, prolife and prochoice alike, frequently express frustration that no matter what they say, their representatives don't listen. They should not be surprised. The abortion debate is so visible and volatile, with such potential for motivating or alienating politically active constituents, that candidates generally have developed an established position before they ever begin to campaign. Once they get into office, they are often deeply indebted to the prolife or prochoice activists who helped elect them and will not risk displeasing those supporters. On such a polarizing issue these candidates will gravitate to one or the other pole (i.e., consistently prolife or consistently prochoice), because the only thing worse than to have one of these groups determined to end your career is to please neither of them.

Activists involved in any high-visibility issue know that it is far easier to elect a candidate who shares their views than to persuade a representative already elected. On lower-profile issues, however, the rules change considerably, as a newly elected Member may take office uncommitted to a position—or even unaware that the issue exists. These representatives may be relatively receptive to constituents who can reach them with intelligent arguments.

Rick Santorum entered Congress with a well-developed philosophy of government that would determine many of his actions. But he claimed no expertise regarding the complexities of the Resolution Trust Corporation, the agency Congress created to handle the assets of failed savings-and-loan institutions. In his first few months he faced a vote on additional funding for the RTC. Lacking sufficient reason to oppose the Bush administration's request for the money, he supported the measure. By the end of that year, constituent complaints about their experiences with the RTC had convinced him that the agency was a fiasco, not a solution, and he was calling for its termination and vowing never again to vote for RTC funding.

I remember the constituent who visited with Congressman Santorum and me to advocate change in the "filed rate doctrine." Not only had we never heard of this issue, but trying to understand it taxed my capacities. The constituent was a transportation broker who made his living by connecting companies needing to send shipments with truckers able to carry those shipments. He could often negotiate rates lower than the official rates those trucking firms were required to file with the federal Interstate Commerce Commission. But when a trucking firm went bankrupt, the bankruptcy trustee and creditors were going back to the brokers (including this constituent) and suing them to recover the difference between the ICC's filed rate and the amount the trucker had actually charged. Courts were holding the brokers responsible for not sticking to the filed rate even though it would seem inconceivable to ask brokers to monitor these filings, many of which changed daily.

Once he understood the issue, Congressman Santorum agreed to support the broker's request for legislative action. This position suited Santorum's general distaste for overly intrusive government regulation of business. But would he have taken a different position had he learned about the issue from a sobbing truck driver whose disability pension was at risk because his company had gone bankrupt after its chief executive awarded too many cut-rate deals to his brother's transportation brokerage?

Sometimes, though probably not in this case, who gets to the Member first can make all the difference. It is neither responsible nor politically wise for a legislator to commit to a position without assessing the opposition's policy arguments and political strength, but sometimes the desire to please a pleading or impatient constituent overrides such prudence.

Nevertheless, in most cases your representative will hear the other side sooner or later, so the caliber and amount of advocacy opposed to you will ultimately become another factor impacting your degree of influence. Accordingly, you can bolster your own case and your credibility by anticipating the main opposing arguments, describing them accurately, refuting them, and (if possible) showing convincingly that you and your friends have more political clout than your opponents. Keep in mind that even the most principled of politicians need to hear political as well as ideological arguments. Elected officials can take only so many unpopular stances if they want to keep their jobs.

Expanding Your Clout
Although the above guidance can help, your influence will never amount to much as long as you remain simply one person with an opinion. To increase your clout you must make yourself either liked or feared.

The best lesson I received in how to make oneself liked came from a culinary arts institute (in more common parlance, a chef school) that invited Congressman Santorum for a tour and lunch shortly after he took office. I had the gastronomic pleasure of tagging along as the aide while the school's president and public-affairs director took us from classroom to classroom, with a prearranged gourmet snack on hand at each stop. Along the way, in addition to building personal rapport with the congressman, they explained how they had made hundreds of students employable, how virtually all of their graduates had found jobs in their field, and how Congress made life difficult for them and other for-profit vocational schools (primarily by narrowing their access to student loans).

I confess that, after enjoying a wonderful lunch at this culinary school, I would have found it hard to vote against their interests on anything. A member of Congress receives multiple sumptuous invitations every day while in Washington, so I think it safe to conclude that the substantive arguments, not the food, exerted lasting influence on Santorum. In any case, this visit played a key role in bringing one member of Congress to the position where, even though he did not sit on any education committees, he frequently would raise his voice when the interests of proprietary schools needed defense.

The school's leaders subsequently availed themselves of the best-known way to become appreciated by a public official: they became financial supporters of Santorum's reelection efforts. The role of money in honest politics deserves considerable attention, and so I will defer that discussion to a later chapter. Suffice it to say, for now, that the more resources you can offer to a campaign, the more that officeholder will appreciate you. But by "resources" I do not mean just money. If you can't contribute financially, you can give volunteer time or help persuade other persons to swing their votes and their influence in the candidate's favor.

Conversely, the more votes and support you can swing *against* candidates whom you dislike, the more influence you wield through inspiring fear. This is the point at which to put to rest the "I'm only one vote" fallacy. True, unless you heed the traditional dictum to "vote early and often" and scurry to multiple voting places forging the signatures of dead persons, you have only one vote. But your spouse has a vote. So do your relatives, friends, neighbors and coworkers. In largely unnoticed local elections, the average person can swing several dozen votes simply by communicating through his or her network of personal relationships. Unresponsive legislative staff members snap out of their doldrums in a hurry when a dissatisfied constituent threatens to tell everyone he knows not to vote for the staffer's boss.

Of course, some threats are more credible than others. Occasionally I have been tempted to invite particularly ill-mannered crackpots to campaign against my boss, on the theory that they would alienate more people than they would convince! You can make yourself more credible than those characters not only by behaving politely but by providing evidence of the other votes you can swing. If you run a business with a hundred employees, a petition signed by those employees, opposing a proposed new tax that would adversely affect your business, shows me that you have the capacity to get their attention on this issue and to inform them whether I am taking their side. If your church names you its legislative liaison and you bring me the monthly issue updates you place in the church bulletin, I will see that you speak potentially for one or two hundred voters. Anyone who sends out a regular newsletter with a specific issue focus and a local mailing list of 200 or more can cause an undecided legislator to take notice, unless the opposing side's newsletter has an even larger circulation.

It is even more impressive if you can demonstrate the ability to activate your network on cue. One friend with an unusually active network of like-minded colleagues was lobbying a state legislator whose staffer made the mistake of commenting, "We really haven't had much public interest in this issue." The next day that office was deluged with 200 calls, and they never again questioned whether my friend represented a sizable constituency.

Building an extensive network takes time and effort. But that is the genius of our democracy, as it serves to represent the people's most deeply felt needs. The amount and caliber of constituent correspondence measures how many people really care about each issue, and the issues arousing the most correspondence rise to top priority. If you can't get more than a handful of citizens actively interested in your cause, you cannot and should not expect legislators to change laws for you.

Establishing a political base—that is, an identifiable group of voters, campaigners or contributors who share your views and follow your leadership—widens your capacity to influence elected officials. If spearheading such an effort is not your cup of tea, at least you should have a greater appreciation of the value of becoming a loyal member and foot soldier in someone else's effort. But either way, as we have noted, it is far more effective to elect candidates who hold your views than to try to shape the views of candidates after they win election. The next chapter will discuss how campaigns work and how you can play an effective role in them.

4

CAMPAIGN FEVER

. . . .

*B*efore I became politically active, I viewed candidates who began running for office two or three years before the election as egocentric, selfish persons too enamored of their own career advancement to be much good. Now I specialize in warning would-be candidates that if they're not willing to start a year or two in advance they shouldn't bother running.

What changed? Was I seduced by overexposure to egomaniacs into thinking like them? I hope not. Rather, I think I have gained, through experience, a more realistic understanding of how campaigns work. But I'll admit that my bias derives in part from working for someone who literally began his campaign for Congress on the day of the previous election.

That's no exaggeration, as I learned one night while sharing a snack with Jon Delano, formerly the top aide to the congressman Rick Santorum defeated in 1990, Doug Walgren. Delano recounted that the day after the 1988 election—in which Walgren coasted to victory, gaining 63 percent of the vote for the third straight time—a friend called him to say, "I know who your next opponent is going to be." While doing his election-day work at the polls as a local Republican committee member, Santorum, regarding a Walgren victory as a certainty, had been telling voters he planned to run in 1990. Before the end of 1988 he had already begun spreading the word among friends and meeting with Republican and civic leaders, launching the single-minded journey that would end in a narrow upset win two years later.

When you finish this chapter you may still think most candidates are egotistical and self-centered, but I hope you will have a clearer sense of what it takes to campaign successfully and why even the most humble, sincere people often must start very early in order to succeed. Whether you wish to run for office yourself, help other candidates, or just become less vulnerable to the styles of campaign persuasion you don't like, a thorough grasp of what makes a good campaign will prove invaluable. For simplicity of expression, portions of this chapter are written as if addressed to the prospective candidate, but anyone who wants to understand or participate in campaigns should find the material relevant.

Before Entering the Starting Gate

Winning an election means reaching the point where, on election day, more voters want you or your candidate as their representative than want anyone else. Even in a local race that may translate to garnering thousands of votes; in a congressional race you may need 100,000 votes to win. If you think a few informative mailings and creative advertising alone can buy those votes, you seriously misunderstand how voters select candidates.

Granted, ads and media coverage play a larger role in statewide races, where a substantial proportion of the populace knows the candidates only through those means of communication. But even then, personal contact with the candidate, or with an enthusiastic campaign worker he or she has inspired, carries far greater impact with most people than do impersonal forms of communication. To reach voters personally you need a network of supporters. The earlier you start, the bigger a network you can build. That, in a nutshell, is why starting early reflects wisdom, not egotism.

In a very real sense, your campaign for office begins long before you declare your candidacy—perhaps even before you dream of being a candidate. It begins with how you live your life every day. Especially at the local level, many voters—particularly the civic-minded ones who in turn will influence their neighbors—will have formed an opinion of you before you start campaigning. They have seen how you treat your children at the town pool or whether you quit coaching the Little League team when your son stopped playing.

A candidate for the school board faces an uphill battle for respect if no one can remember anything that person has done to assist the school district or learn how it functions. Conversely, a successful campaign is often the culmination of years or decades of public service and building friendships with people who will say, with an unshakable conviction based on firsthand experience, "She's the kind of person I want representing me."

Along with personal relationships and reputations, candidates also enter the campaign starting gate with résumés that will help or hurt their cause. You can selectively describe your background, but you can't fabricate it; nor can you conceal its politically undesirable components, for your opponent is likely to uncover them. Thus some otherwise qualified prospective candidates are excluded or severely disadvantaged by the "baggage" of their past lives. A paper trail of prior writings or recorded statements that sound extreme virtually ensures defeat.

To take an obvious contemporary example: Pat Robertson's career as a religious broadcaster and writer, while endearing him to millions of supporters, is also his greatest political drawback. His detractors repeatedly use certain of his on-the-record statements (such as his claim to have diverted a hurricane from Virginia Beach through prayer) to make him sound too far out of the American cultural mainstream. In my judgment, the most amazing aspect of Robertson's 1988 presidential campaign was not its collapse but how far he succeeded before flopping on the "Super Tuesday" when most of the Southern states hold their primaries. Keep in mind, however, that Robertson's victories occurred in Republican caucuses and primaries, not in a general election. In a similar situation, national home-schooling leader Mike Farris captured the Republican nomination for lieutenant governor of Virginia in 1993 but succumbed to the predictable attacks on his "extreme Religious Right" views in that November's election.

I do not mean to suggest that a politically undesirable background proves that person's inferiority; it may hint at just the reverse. Sometimes the voices we most need to hear are those of provocative, uncompromising persons who could never win a popular election, and the alternative outlets for those voices—such as think tanks, syndicated columns, college professorships, church pastorates and nonprofit advocacy organizations—are in no way lesser callings than elected office. However, if you do think you may ever want to run for office, be cautious about what you say or write and with whom you associate. Potential candidates carefully avoid unpopular or extremist causes while seeking to establish civic respectability through public service, charitable activity or board memberships (preferably well in advance of the campaign, lest the service appear politically motivated).

I dwell on this point so as to underscore the truth that a campaign is more than meets the casual observer's eye. It is less a contest of dueling media consultants, and more a reflection of individuals' ability to establish their character and credibility, than uninvolved citizens realize. And I suspect that this misconception discourages many persons who are not media wizards or big-money fundraisers from becoming more active in the political process. A candidate does need money and media help, of course, but a campaign has many other pieces too. Let's see how they fit together in the whole picture.

Hitting the Road

First, since there is no substitute for personal contact, the candidate wants to talk personally with as many people as possible. Often he or she will spend hours going door to door for this purpose. Door-to-door campaigning shows people you care enough to call on them personally; it contacts people who might not be reached any other way; and it generates trust and enthusiasm by projecting the image of a tireless, hard-working campaigner.

Rick Santorum perfected the art of door-to-door campaigning in his first run for Congress. To conserve the time wasted by knocking on unanswered doors, volunteers walked each side of the street, leaving literature where no one was home and calling the candidate to the door if someone answered. They also carried lists of registered voters and kept a record of the persons with whom they spoke, so that the campaign office could follow up with personalized letters. When distributing literature in my own neighborhood on the weekend before the election, I experienced an unforgettable verification of this effort's success. On the streets where Santorum had not gone door to door I received a mixed response, but on the streets he had personally visited, the support was overwhelming, with many residents offering unsolicited, favorable comments on the impression he had made when he came to their door *six months earlier.*

In more rural areas door-to-door "blitzes" can be effective. A county, state or federal candidate's campaign visit to a small town can be big news—at least big enough to be mentioned in the local newspaper. Here the candidate might recruit volunteers to divide up streets and cover a whole community in a single day, distributing literature and inviting residents to meet the candidate at a public forum that evening.

The mechanics of door-to-door campaigning begin to illustrate the importance of mobilizing human, not just financial, resources: the candidate who can recruit and organize volunteer help greatly increases his or her effectiveness. The more opportunities you have to communicate your side of the story—positive information about your candidate and negative information about the opposition—the better chance you have to win.

Even so, door-to-door activity is inefficient in several ways. It entails considerable effort and planning to reach just one or two persons at a time. To catch most people at home, one must visit during evenings or weekends, when many other events compete for the candidate's time and attention. And unless a campaign volunteer knows the neighborhood's residents extremely well, these visits are "cold calls" in the sense that one doesn't know how to appeal best to the person who opens the door—what values that person holds or what concerns are most important to him or her. (Even if you ask, you will usually get brief and noncommittal answers. Candidates whom I have counseled frequently are surprised that, when they go door to door, hardly anyone wants to talk with them about any issue.) These inefficiencies suggest the benefits of several alternative modes of campaigning.

Locating the Crowds
First, the candidate can often interact with hundreds of voters

at once by attending public events such as parades, community days or high-school football games. Such events maximize the opportunity for personal, albeit usually superficial, contacts as well as showing the candidate's interest in the local community. Generally, since everyone knows candidates must attend major community events, one does not so much win new friends by showing up as one risks losing support by being conspicuously absent. But one can get a lot of mileage out of a personal appearance at an event of importance to the participants, like an ethnic or veterans group's annual banquet or a church supper. Again, this depends on the candidate's success in motivating supporters to provide information about these events and, ideally, increase credibility by personally introducing him or her to those in attendance. At large public events like parades and football games, even if the candidate cannot be present personally, volunteers can still pass out campaign literature to the crowd.

I vividly recall the occasion three weeks before election day when a woman highly respected in her community told Congressman Santorum to meet her at the Methodist church's ham loaf dinner the following evening. A packed schedule of Saturday campaigning was rearranged, and Santorum spent an hour traveling from table to table, greeting over two hundred people. Two weeks later, when we made final please-vote-for-Rick phone calls to people in that town, several of them commented on having met the candidate at their church dinner. I have no doubt that that appearance won the votes of dozens of people who did not pay attention to national issues and for whom that evening was their only exposure to any candidate.

A second approach is to secure any public-speaking appearance possible, such as a Rotary or Lions Club luncheon or a Chamber of Commerce breakfast, where the candidate can put his best foot forward by making a presentation to an assembled group. However, such civic groups usually seek to maintain political neutrality by declining candidates as speakers unless they invite all candidates. Even worse, some of them reinforce incumbents' already high reelection rates by inviting the current officeholder to address their group (in his official status as a legislator) but not offering challengers an equal platform.

Therefore, candidates frequently resort to arranging their own events. One of the most common of these is the "coffee." Here a supporter invites friends and neighbors to his or her home for an evening with the candidate, who gives a brief presentation, answers questions and mingles with those attending. The invitations themselves increase the candidate's name recognition even among recipients who cannot attend.

My experience suggests that the coffee host should invite five to ten times as many persons as the desired attendance—and then persistently follow up written invitations with phone calls. Trying to pull off this kind of event always seems to teach neophytes, who promise a crowd of thirty persons but end up with five or ten, the level of citizen apathy that pervades even their closest friends. Nevertheless, even a small coffee is usually worth the candidate's time, because those who attend have greater than average interest, and a good presentation to a receptive audience can turn half or more of the listeners into active supporters. Admittedly, to spend an evening with ten or twenty persons when you ultimately need 100,000 votes feels like a tiny step forward, but it takes time to win people's energetic, committed support—and, once energized, these people will spread the word to many others. (Again, that's why you start early!)

Targeting the Key Players

To reach those persons most likely to influence the result of an election, a candidate must take a more direct approach. Who are these persons? The first obvious group is the officials and local committee members of the candidate's political party. Their endorsement and active support can be crucial in a primary election and usually form the core of a successful candidate's campaign in a general election. Candidates or their representatives will visit the party meetings in their communities month after month, because they know that these are the people most likely to become very involved in a campaign.

A second key category of potentially influential participants is leaders identified with one or more of the issues the candidate must address. In almost any policy area, one can find groups that specialize in analyzing those issues, educating the public on that group's views, and seeking to elect candidates who agree with the group. For example, a candidate with a strong commitment to environmental protection will want to meet local leaders of the Sierra Club and Audubon Society and secure their permission to communicate his or her views to group members through a regular meeting, the organization's newsletter or a special mailing. That candidate will probably choose not to contact other leaders, such as representatives of the lumber or waste-disposal industries, who curse environmentalists for reducing their industry's profits.

A third key category includes anyone who might give your campaign a large chunk of money. There's no way around it— every campaign needs money, and very seldom, unless the candidate is personally wealthy, does it have all the money it could use. If you can't stand looking people in the eye and asking them for a contribution, don't run for office. If you do run, you will want to compile a list of likely donors and their reasons for giving— whether they support all good Democratic candidates, or pro-business candidates, or alumni from your university. Then you will want to give them whatever attention or information is needed to secure their support. If you do not know the solicitation target personally, someone who does should make an introductory call in advance, so as to establish your credibility. Whenever a well-heeled contributor commits support to you, ask whom that person in turn can call on your behalf.

What Do You Talk About?

All of this adds up to a lot of talking to a lot of people about a lot of issues. To make a good impression, you have to sound intelligent on all of them. I believe issue development is the most difficult piece of the campaign puzzle. A good candidate must be able not only to articulate a position on each issue but to express those positions in a way that shows understanding of the law and of current policy debates.

In most situations, just being able to articulate a position is as important as what position you take. A candidate for state legislature might face, in a typical coffee, questions on a dozen different issues, ranging from education to taxes to insurance regulation. Some of the questions may cover matters of interest to no one in the audience except the questioner. But if you come across as uninformed about any issue, your listeners will doubt your preparedness. One insurance agent who catches you off guard with a question about state law, or one hospital administrator who wonders why you aren't aware that your proposal for children's health coverage was tried in a neighboring state three years ago and failed miserably, can ruin an otherwise good appearance.

In my judgment, the task of issue development is insurmountable in a single leap. Don't try to run for the school board if you haven't been involved in your school system for at least two years; not only will your sudden ambition be suspect, but you will probably betray your lack of background knowledge when you start campaigning. However, neither must you become an encyclopedia before you begin to pursue a candidacy. A general knowledge of the major issues, such as one can glean from attending a few meetings or consistently reading local papers or weekly newsmagazines, should suffice to get you started. If you know enough on an issue to have decided who your allies will be, you can ask them to provide you with the facts, figures and arguments to help you defend their positions.

By the time you become a declared candidate, you should have developed firm stances, preferably accompanied by policy papers, on the eight or ten issues of greatest concern. This homework, plus a general knowledge of the recent activities of the legislative body or executive office to which you seek election, should help you navigate any public appearance without too many embarrassing admissions of ignorance. Then, when someone does hit you with an obscure inquiry—say, wondering if you support legislation to overturn a recent court ruling that expanded coal miners' pension rights—you can take the opportunity to broaden your own knowledge base: "I honestly can't say I've looked at that issue, but if you'll stick around afterward I'd be happy to hear your concerns and see if I can support your position."

Keep in mind that on even the hottest issues only a small minority is mobilized on either side, while the silent majority is not ideologically motivated and will side with whoever reaches them with an intelligent-sounding appeal, regardless of its content. This fact underscores the central importance of getting your message out by all means possible—personal campaigning, volunteer help, earned media (i.e., news coverage) and paid media (direct mail and advertising)—for whoever communicates with the most people will usually win, no matter what he or she is saying. It also reminds you, when confronted with a question from an implacable opponent, to aim your response not at the questioner but at the majority of your listeners who have not taken sides. You need only half the votes plus one to win, so you want to spend your time swaying the "uncommitted middle" to your side, not trading barbs with the handful who are already

61

committed to opposing you no matter what you say.

What Do You Want People to Do for You?

Once you have recruited supporters, what do you ask them to do? Some of the answers have been suggested already: give money, host coffees, tell friends, assist in the campaign office and with mailings, go door to door. Other support functions deserve further discussion, as these roles shed light on the mechanics of a successful campaign.

Phoning. One of the best ways to make personal contact with a large number of voters on a candidate's behalf is through an organized system of phone calls. The local board of elections can supply a list of registered voters in each town, arranged by voting district (we refer to them as "street lists," also used for door-to-door visits and literature deliveries). If you can afford to buy the software or an expensive directory, you can get a fancier list with phone numbers included; if not, someone will have to look up the numbers.

The simplest phoning approach is to have volunteers phone as many voters as possible during the week before the election with a *brief* (so as to remain inoffensive) message urging them to vote for your candidate. You may want to have volunteers come to a "phone bank" (i.e., a central location with many outgoing phone lines available) to make their calls, marking off the homes they reach and leaving the lists for the next volunteers when they have to quit. Alternatively, if you feel you can trust volunteers to make a specified set of calls without supervision, you can give them lists and have them work at home.

These calls can be surprisingly effective, and their persuasiveness may be increasing as it becomes harder in our society to recruit volunteers to do anything. They can produce in sympathetic or uncommitted voters an appreciative response of "if she's willing to spend her evenings making calls for Representative

Jones, the least I can do is go out and vote for him."

If you lack the volunteer resources to phone all voters, you may want to improve your efficiency by phoning only those most likely to respond favorably, such as those registered with your candidate's party (in a general election) or members of organizations that support the candidate. In this case the phone script can be tailored to fit the group targeted, and callers can streamline the message by assuming the persons targeted are supportive of the candidate; their goal is simply to get the people out to vote. Casual observers forget that many elections are won not so much by changing minds as by getting your supporters to the polls on election day. The national Republican tide in 1994 resulted as much because angry Republicans were more motivated to vote than disillusioned Democrats as it did from any significant change in popular opinion.

If you have enough volunteers you can expand the phoning system, making initial calls three to six weeks before the election. In these calls, you describe the candidate you're supporting in one or two sentences and ask voters if they have made up their minds yet. When someone expresses support for your candidate, mark that person "favorable" and call back just before election day with a reminder to vote. Thank the unfavorables for their time and hang up praying that they forget to vote. Send undecided voters your best piece of campaign literature with a handwritten note like "I hope this will help you make up your mind," and try to call back during the final week to ask if they need any more information to convince them to back your candidate.

Another common variation is the negative phone appeal, often used on behalf of a challenger seeking to undermine the popularity of a well-known incumbent. These calls may take the form of a polling survey in order to communicate negative information: "Does the fact that Congressman Smith voted to raise your taxes eighteen times in the last four years make you more likely, somewhat less likely, or much less likely to vote for him?" In a low-budget campaign this amateur phoning *becomes* the poll, helping the candidate determine which criticisms of the opponent will be most effective.

It all sounds easy—and it is, if you can find and organize the reliable volunteers to do it. At two hundred calls per volunteer, it takes a thousand volunteers, each willing to offer ten hours of their time, to blanket a congressional district with phone calls. More threateningly, the apathy, desire for privacy, and loss of civility currently pervading our culture can make campaigning by phone an unpleasant experience marked by hostile respondents. You may find more than a few volunteers offering to do office work, pass out literature—*anything* other than phone calls.

Yard signs and bumper stickers. I used to think yard signs were useless. Why should a bunch of signs with no information beyond the candidate's name affect my vote? Well, they're not useless. They establish a candidate's name recognition, which makes voters more attuned to additional information about that candidate. They also establish credibility by giving the impression of broad support. In putting a sign on my property I make a statement to neighbors, friends and anyone else who knows where I live, drives by my house and respects my judgment. (Therefore, never give anyone a yard sign who is hated by his neighbors.) Bumper stickers perform a similar function, sometimes better than yard signs if the persons you can most influence are more likely to see your car (e.g., at work or in a church parking lot) than your house.

Poll workers. Your campaign's last major grassroots activity (unless this is illegal in your area) will be the recruitment of volunteers to stand at polling places and hand out cards bearing your candidate's name to incoming voters. If everyone decided how to vote before coming to the polls, we could all be spared running the gauntlet of poll workers zealously making a final effort to

64

persuade the electorate. In highly publicized elections nearly everyone does decide in advance, and thus you will seldom see a poll worker for a presidential candidate. But in local races a significant number of voters may arrive at the polls not even knowing who their choices are—and may very well vote for the person whose literature they received when entering the building.

During the 1992 Santorum campaign I performed an unscientific experiment. Early on the Sunday morning before election day I traveled to a low-income community where a smashing 4 percent of the voters are registered Republican and distributed Santorum campaign literature in one precinct. Along with a friend, I covered that precinct's voting place on election day, while another friend passed out Santorum cards at another precinct (where I had not distributed literature) and a third was not covered at all. Comparing the election returns between precincts suggested that, on this occasion, a poll worker could swing 5 to 10 percent of the votes in our candidate's direction, while literature distribution plus a poll worker could alter perhaps 15 percent of the votes. (And remember, this was a race for Congress, not for some obscure local post.) Poll workers may also have greater value in less highly educated communities, where they can actually engage relatively uninformed voters in last-minute conversations, than in white-collar areas where well-read, busy professionals rush past, ignoring the poll worker.

How It All Works

Thorough campaign manuals contain hundreds of pages; this chapter can only summarize key components of a campaign. I have omitted countless fine points of grassroots campaigning, such as always having an open-air automobile available for parades along with balloons or candy to hand out to children. I have not touched on more technical aspects, such as how to identify "swing voters" most likely to cross party lines or how to develop

65

a consistent, favorable image of the candidate in media appearances and debates, as these decisions are generally reserved for professional experts. I have tried, however, to detail the main areas of essential campaign activity to which persons deciding whether and how to support a candidate may be exposed. My first campaign experience, in which Rick Santorum emerged from nowhere to narrowly oust an incumbent congressman, has become a model of sorts in national Republican circles and, accordingly, should serve as a helpful illustration of how all these activities can come together.

Santorum began constructing his campaign two years in advance, drawing on his experience as an aide to a state legislator and the relationships he had built as a lawyer and party activist. During the first year (1989) he solidified his base by holding private meetings, calling on party leaders and visiting with local Republican committees. By the end of that year he had recruited volunteer grassroots coordinators for most of the communities in the district and had raised about $50,000, a modest sum by congressional standards but enough to bankroll expanded activities. Names of volunteers were entered into a database, coded by location and by what duties they were willing to perform.

In January 1990 Santorum hired a staff member to manage the grassroots effort. He also began curtailing his law practice, which he left completely in April in order to campaign full time. By analyzing data from past campaigns, he identified the areas with the most swing voters—areas where some Republicans had done far better than others, indicating that spirited campaigning could make a big difference. He concentrated his door-to-door efforts on these localities. Meanwhile, a volunteer scheduler scoured local papers to spot parades, community events and dinners the candidate could attend, as well as arranging coffees and meetings with prospective supporters.

Having spent many years studying national issues, Santorum

was well prepared on this score and released a handful of brief position statements when he officially announced his candidacy in late January. He saved money by securing the volunteer services of an inexperienced but energetic press secretary (me), who expedited the production of additional position papers (usually drafted by one of Santorum's friends with expertise in that area) and one or two press releases each week. These releases often appeared in the news-starved suburban newspapers and bolstered his credibility with major media sources as a well-informed candidate, causing them to treat him more respectfully when they began covering the race seriously in its last few weeks.

Santorum targeted groups he knew to be dissatisfied with incumbent congressman Doug Walgren, including prolife advocates, sportsmen and some business groups, for donations and volunteer support. Meanwhile he contracted with a polling service to find out what issues were most important to the congressional district's voters, where they stood on those issues, and which themes could most effectively arouse general discontent with the incumbent. Santorum discovered that his opponent's two most vulnerable points were his support for congressional pay increases and his practice of maintaining his primary residence in Washington while seldom returning to his district.

To capitalize on this information, while continuing his daily effort to build a network of supporters through personal contact, Santorum began running radio and television ads during the summer, attacking Walgren on the issues of pay raises and residency. Advertising time on major television stations was prohibitively expensive, so Santorum's media consultant reserved time on cable television broadcasts of Pittsburgh Pirates baseball games—getting a big bang for the buck as the Pirates unexpectedly soared toward their first division title in nine years. (Perhaps you never realized that a baseball team could help to decide an election!) In what most observers considered a tactical error,

Walgren, rather than simply trumpeting his own record and ignoring his opponent, ran response ads attacking Santorum by name, thus creating the impression of a potentially tight race and giving the upstart challenger more name recognition than he could afford to purchase himself.

Slowly but surely, Santorum's support snowballed as enthusiastic supporters—most of whom he had reached personally through door-knocking, coffees and issue-based outreaches—spread the word about him, called talk shows and wrote letters to local papers. A protracted budget battle in Congress, finally resolved less than two weeks before election day, added to public dissatisfaction with the status quo while keeping Walgren stuck in Washington. Congress adjourned just in time to allow Walgren to return home for the one formal debate in which he had agreed to participate; with little time to prepare, he seemed uncertain and disorganized in trying to fend off Santorum's aggressive attacks.

In a final burst of enthusiasm, the Santorum campaign recruited college students to hold large banners along Pittsburgh's main roads at rush hour. Meanwhile a last mailing, targeted at Democrats considered likely to vote for Republicans, pointedly highlighted Walgren's identified weaknesses. On election day Santorum won 51.4 percent of the vote, a success directly attributable to the enthusiasm he had generated: 73 percent of the registered Republicans in the district voted, compared to only 56 percent of the Democrats.

You Can Have an Impact

Even in victory, the Santorum campaign provided a reminder of how difficult it is to dislodge an incumbent: powered by a combination of very hard work and a multiplicity of good breaks, Santorum could manage only a narrow win. (The success rate for U.S. House members seeking reelection in 1990 exceeded 96 percent.) But it also showed that, even at the congressional level, *campaigns remain within the average person's sphere of influence.* Santorum won mainly through his own tireless campaigning and that of several hundred active volunteers. His mailings and ads certainly helped, but he lacked the funds to advertise on major Pittsburgh television stations until the last weekend before election day.

When David Price, a Duke University political science professor first elected to Congress from North Carolina in 1986, wrote a book about his experiences, he described his first three campaigns largely in terms of dueling television ads, along with the sophisticated polling that helped him decide which ads to run. He may be accurately assessing the main factors in his own races, as well as many others covering large states or spacious districts in which most voters see the candidates mainly through their paid advertising. In fact, as campaigns despair of locating adequate numbers of reliable volunteers and turn more heavily toward dependence on fundraising, paid staff, paid advertising and media attention, those willing to help at the grassroots level often discover there is nothing for them to do. In other races, however, grassroots communication on the candidate's behalf can make all the difference. Personal communication by convinced backers to their friends and neighbors builds the firm support that an opponent's attack ads cannot undermine.

You may feel your support for a candidate can't matter very much. But the bigger the personal network you build, in terms of voters and financial contributors who respond to your recommendation, the more help you can deliver to a campaign and the more your support will be coveted. Over time you may reach the point where, rather than just evaluating a candidate and deciding whether to back him or her, you may actually be called upon to help candidates develop their positions.

Even if you never want to progress to that level of clout, a good grasp of campaign mechanics and a modest investment of time can make you a reliable and prized volunteer. Like successful military campaigns, political campaigns need well-trained, loyal soldiers. By serving as one such soldier, you can do more than you might think to advance the causes you value.

5

TEMPTATIONS
HONEST
POLITICIANS FACE

. . . .

When John Jackley turned from congressional aide to author, Capitol Hill blushed. Jackley kept a voluminous journal while toiling on three congressional staffs during the 1980s, and the book he wrote upon his departure, *Hill Rat*, paints an ugly picture of Washington politics as viewed from within.

Jackley depicted members of Congress who cast votes strictly for the purpose of enhancing their reelection chances, or who viewed the tragic death of a constituent as an opportunity to gain favorable media coverage by demanding an investigation. He told of youthful staff, intoxicated by power, who worked to carve out their own fiefdoms of authority and who took pleasure in using their position to rudely demand action from high-level agency officials twice their age. Jackley's exposé does not inspire confidence in how Congress leads our nation.

My colleagues and I sometimes joked about whether I would write a sequel, from the perspective of a district office, to *Hill Rat*. Indeed, one can experience plenty of dirty politics without going to Washington. However, I prefer to see the cup as half-full rather than half-empty. While many politicians engage in dishonest and self-serving activity, most maintain a level of honesty and integrity befitting a civic leader.

Nevertheless, even many of those who enter politics with clean hearts go astray in the course of their careers. Politics offers uniquely acute temptations—power, money, fame, adulation. It also presents dilemmas of increasing complexity that can gradually, imperceptibly cause well-meaning public servants to lose their ethical moorings, adequately justifying their decisions to themselves along the way without ever realizing what they have lost.

It's easy to stand outside the system and say you could serve in politics without compromising your integrity—but what constitutes a breach of integrity? Consider the following situations:

☐ You represent a district in woeful need of a new highway system. When you lobby the chairman of the transportation committee to include this project in the committee's appropriations, he agrees to push it through—if and only if you support his proposed gas tax increase, which you have not publicly criticized but which you consider to be bad policy.

☐ A prominent local businessman offers to arrange a major fundraising event for your campaign, on the simple condition that once in office you strongly urge a state agency to drop its costly investigation of his business's labor practices. After all, this investigation could mean lost jobs in your town.

☐ You are about to vote on a new mandate to be levied on small businesses in your state. You believe the mandate is bad policy, but you also know that a vote against it will enable your opponent

72

to mobilize unions to campaign against you in the election three months away. You know that the measure will pass despite your opposition. So does the local Chamber of Commerce director, who assures you that all the business people she represents will understand and, in fact, want you to "throw a bone to the unions" on this vote so as to remain in office and help to protect the business community's long-term interests.

☐ You are a Republican president battling a Democratic Congress over a long-delayed budget agreement for the coming fiscal year. The Democrats insist on sending you a bill that includes tax increases. Your lips tell you to veto any such bill, lest you be accused of breaking a highly visible campaign promise. (Remember "Read my lips—no new taxes"?) But if you resist a compromise, government operations will run out of funds and you will be blamed for everything from nonpayment of federal employees to closing the Washington Monument and Yosemite National Park.

Most outsiders fail to recognize the complexity of the judgment calls politicians must make every day. Yet I remain convinced that political success does not require abandonment of principle. Let's look at a few of the most tempting areas of moral compromise and how the honest politician can deal with them.

If You Get Me a Job . . .

"I just submitted an application to the State Transportation Department. If you can get me a position there, you can rest assured that I'll remember your boss the next time he needs campaign workers."

When I began my political service I was unprepared for the frequency with which requests like this one would come in. Nor did I realize several other factors that compound this moral dilemma. First, constituents are often grossly misinformed about the powers of a legislator's office. Either they criticize you for not pulling strings to get them a job when their score on the civil-service test does not qualify them for an interview, or they thank you profusely for sending a boilerplate "please consider this applicant" letter that you know will have no impact. Second, on some occasions I really could get someone an interview (though not a job) just by virtue of my phone call on a legislator's behalf. Third, it is frightfully easy to deceive the constituent; for example, an aide can provide the applicant a glowing recommendation letter praising his character and experience and then phone the agency's personnel office to explain that the letter was written out of political necessity and should be ignored.

Furthermore, I did not realize how many people in American government still owe their jobs to good old political patronage. A top administrator in the county where I live once stated unabashedly that he (on behalf of the county commissioners) controlled 1,500 patronage jobs, in addition to countless no-bid professional service contracts for which campaign contributors get the inside track. Those in power maintain their position by delivering government jobs and contracts in exchange for political support. During one campaign in which I was involved, an anonymous caller identified himself as a county employee and stated, "I've just done my job—putting up yard signs for your opponent—but they can't steal my vote." (In the interest of fairness, let me hasten to state that although the bosses in my county were Democrats, similar scenes occur under many Republican administrations. The temptation to abuse power is nonpartisan.)

I cannot stomach this type of patronage, for it manipulates public resources for personal benefit. But there is also an honest kind of patronage, best illustrated by the role of legislative staff. Any intelligent legislator makes political loyalty a top criterion in staff hiring decisions, and I have often told persons aspiring to political employment that they should start by campaigning their tails off for the candidates of their choice.

The distinction between honest and inappropriate patronage hinges on whether political allegiance is indeed a bona fide qualification for the job at hand. Any posts that entail developing or advocating an elected official's policies should go to persons who support that official and have a stake in his or her continued success. In contrast, the effectiveness of the transportation department's road repair crew or the building inspector is unrelated to those employees' political views, and as a result such positions should be awarded on the basis of competence, not favoritism.

How, then, does the honest politician handle job seekers without offending them? I always sought to distinguish between a letter of reference and a letter of consideration. Every time an official writes a letter of reference, I explained, he puts his own credibility on the line; as a result, we could give a substantive recommendation only to the degree that we were personally familiar with the applicant's character or abilities (or had received a reference from someone else whose judgment we trusted). Even if we had the power to tell an agency or employer whom to hire, I would explain, we would not use it. I would then always offer to submit a letter of consideration, requesting that the constituent's application receive a full and careful review.

In this way the constituent always felt he or she was receiving something of value (namely, our office's assistance in ensuring that the application was not overlooked or lost). I had a form letter on file for this purpose, noting that the constituent's "initiative in contacting me illustrates a strong interest in this position" (a good diplomat can put the best face on almost anything). Constituents seemed appreciative of this effort—even if inwardly chastened by the rebuff of their pursuit of a political favor—especially since, having known myself the humiliation of wandering the streets in search of work, I had particular compassion for the unemployed and took the time to connect them with any relevant sources of job-search assistance.

Whereas pestering your favorite politician probably won't get you a job, doing good politics can certainly help—and not only with jobs in government. Experienced employment counselors know that effective high-level networking beats reading want ads as a way to locate good jobs, and politics is perhaps the best place to do such networking. By hanging around campaign and polit-ical-party functions, you will meet leaders from many sectors of your community in a context where you make a favorable impres-sion just by being there. I didn't enter politics to advance my career, but when I voluntarily exited government service I sud-denly realized that an extraordinary number of influential per-sons were available to open doors for me; rather than having to deal with the gatekeepers at a company's personnel department, I could just call my friend who ran the company. And it didn't hurt to have a U.S. Senator as a personal reference. If I only enjoyed the work of a lobbyist, I'd be set for life.

Let's Make a Deal

The sample ethical dilemmas I offered at the beginning of this chapter all derive from the nature of democratic politics as an exercise in perpetual dealmaking. I remember hearing a state legislator lament the early retirement of an honorable colleague who had grown tired of having to cut a deal every time he wanted to accomplish something. Clean politicians uncomfortable with this necessity often seem to feel trapped: they feel corrupt if they play along and doomed to ineffectiveness if they don't.

Dealmaking is not inherently evil, however; it depends on what deals you make. Each legislator enters the dealmaking game with an intangible amount of legitimate clout—composed of such items as votes, staff resources, responsibility for committee deci-sions, campaign funds, the potential to attract media attention and the ability to advance a few select funding requests each year—and can expend or trade on this account in a myriad of ways, many of them perfectly appropriate.

Let's look at a few examples. Suppose the majority and minority parties are sharply divided on a particular piece of legislation. The minority cannot defeat a unified majority on the final vote, but it has other forms of clout. For instance, minority party members may threaten to make the majority's lack of bipartisanship an issue during the next campaign season if no compromise versions of this legislation are offered. Or they may vow to reject all compromises the next time the majority party is not unified and needs cooperation from minority members to pass a bill. As a result, the majority may offer a compromise even though they had the votes to pass the original version. In response, minority members may agree to vote for legislation about which they are not enthusiastic. They have not sold their votes; rather, they have used their available influence to secure, from their perspective, a better legislative result than they could have achieved without making the deal.

When President Clinton sought to round up the votes in Congress to pass the North American Free Trade Agreement (NAFTA) in 1993, he was accused of offering special favors to wavering lawmakers in exchange for their support. If he offered deals not germane to the issue at hand (e.g., "Vote for NAFTA and I'll make sure your city gets a new bridge"), he can rightly be charged with illegitimate dealmaking. However, when he offered related concessions (such as exemptions or special trade protection for certain industries), he was simply making alterations designed to help more lawmakers conclude that, on balance, they could support the bill.

I believe the honest politician can distinguish legitimate from illegitimate compromise by asking whether he or she is prepared to present a true explanation in defense of the actions. Would a minority-party legislative leader be willing to state publicly, "I opposed the initial version of this bill but promised the majority my support if two provisions were dropped"? Of course. That is legitimate, substantive negotiation. But how about "I opposed this education bill at first but said I would support it if they promised me an extra million dollars of funding to repair the state park in my district"? That line probably wouldn't qualify for the legislator's press release. If a compromise sounds *compromising* to the public, it's not the right thing to do in private.

Politicians shouldn't need to engage in underhanded dealmaking, because there are plenty of things they can offer in good conscience. For example, they can promise to campaign for (or abstain from campaigning against) a colleague; they can commit to making some issue or project a higher priority; they can agree to do behind-the-scenes committee work that will advance the colleague's leadership potential or public image. Legislators are so busy that time, energy and attention become valued commodities, so one can often negotiate by offering to intensify or prioritize one's already-held commitments rather than by betraying one's conscience.

Many seem to believe that politics is inevitably dirty due to the compromises required. Good politics is indeed an exercise in continual compromise—but so is my marriage. Politics needs not purists who refuse to make deals, but responsible persons with principle and depth who can discern which deals are appropriate.

Getting Reelected

"If you can't get reelected, you won't get anything done down here." Rick Santorum says that was virtually the opening statement at the orientation session he attended as a newly elected congressman. The statement is essentially true, especially in a system where seniority brings so much clout. But it also explains why elected officials sometimes seem to have no higher goal than their own reelection. If everything you do depends on getting reelected, then why not do whatever it takes to gain reelection?

I believe we desperately need leaders who value righteousness over career advancement—who will do the right thing even if it means losing their jobs. In fairness to those much-maligned politicians, however, we should recall that we do not expect people in any other field to take steps that will endanger their own position. It should not be surprising, therefore, that only under immense political pressure will most legislators vote to reduce their staff allotment or their mailing privileges, or that twenty-year veteran legislators seldom support term limits.

Permitting incumbent legislators to set their own office budgets and write campaign laws invites such an obvious conflict of interest, in my judgment, that I would prefer to see these matters assigned to a special nonpartisan commission. Even if we make exceptions for this area, though, we will find that political calculations play a larger role in many lawmakers' votes than the public realizes.

And I don't mean just the simple consideration of whether a vote will be popular back home in the district. The intrigues of party caucuses get far more complex. Behind the closed doors of party caucus meetings, legislators, especially the newest members, are warned to fall in line with what the party leadership wants, or else. (The "or else" may mean termination of a government program in the rebel legislator's district, an unwanted committee assignment, reduction of her office budget, or lack of party support for her next campaign.) On key, controversial votes party leaders will demand loyalty until they know they have enough votes to win. At that point, which legislators are permitted to vote against the leadership may be determined not by who most strongly opposes the bill, but by who most needs to cast a "nay" vote in order to survive the next election.

And politicians have other tricks in their repertoires. On bills they know will be decided by a lopsided vote, they may "throw a bone" to a particular interest group, voting in that group's favor so as to pacify it or at least shield themselves against its criticism. They monitor special-interest-group scorecards and try to cast just enough votes with each group to avoid being targeted for defeat by any of them. Party leaders carefully scheme to bring certain amendments up during floor debate on a bill, so that members can tell one lobbying interest that they supported the bill while pointing out to the other side that they backed the amendments aimed at weakening the bill. Since few people outside government understand these tricks, a skillful politician can satisfy (dupe?) almost everyone, to the painful dismay of the challenger he or she will swamp in the next election.

These practices are so commonplace, and the pressures of political considerations so prevalent, that no one can realistically hope to avoid them completely. In fact, a good legislative aide keeps the boss attentive to political concerns; one of Congressman Santorum's staff earned the nickname "Lefty" for his efforts to soften some of Santorum's more conservative stances. Nevertheless, as I argued regarding compromises, I think it is realistic to ask legislators never to take a position they cannot honestly defend.

This ethical guideline still leaves lawmakers plenty of latitude, since so many votes are judgment calls with good arguments on both sides. A legislator concerned about a low rating from the Chamber of Commerce need not "throw them a bone"; he can send his aide to Chamber headquarters with the task of comparing legislative agendas and identifying the areas of agreement where they can work together. Almost inevitably there will be some common concerns which the legislator can then elevate to a higher priority on his own agenda. On the rare occasions where there is no common ground whatsoever, the Member can take his zero rating from the Chamber of Commerce and wear it as a badge of honor when seeking campaign help from unions. In politics every cloud, unless it carries the sting of moral reproach, has a silver lining.

Representing a Constituency

The issue of how political considerations affect a legislator's vote raises a commonly asked question. How should an elected official reflect his or her constituents' views? There are two extreme answers to this question, both of them wrong.

One extreme argues that a representative should follow the majority opinion in the district on every issue. This view ignores the difference between *pure* democracy (which would result if we put every issue to a national referendum) and *representative* democracy, in which we periodically elect representatives who decide the issues on our behalf. Pure democracy is undesirable for several reasons. First, the people we choose to represent us have access to more information, as well as more time and resources to study the issues, than we have. In some cases (most notably, matters related to defense or national security) their decisions are based heavily on classified information they cannot reveal to the public. Furthermore, many of their decisions call for moral judgment, not for automatic conformity to prevailing opinion. Any leader who aligns her position on a proposed military action or capital punishment or abortion with whatever more than half of her constituents believe is not morally fit for leadership. (I do not wish to imply that the only decisions requiring moral judgment are the explicitly life-and-death ones; these are simply the most obvious examples.)

The other extreme, which argues that a truly upright representative should simply follow his or her conscience without regard to public opinion, ignores several facts about the nature of representation. First, an elected official functions not as a neutral arbiter but as advocate for the people who elect him or her. In the U.S. House of Representatives, for example, only one of 435 members is charged with looking after my community's needs. That does not mean my member of Congress should automatically endorse every project his constituents propose; his clout can go only so far, and if he advocates for bad projects he will lose the credibility he needs to advance the good ones. But once my congressman determines what are the most pressing transportation needs in suburban Pittsburgh, I expect him to support them forcefully for federal funding and to let others determine whether the projects sought by Detroit or Denver deserve higher priority.

Second, many of a legislator's decisions entail choosing among various good causes rather than passing moral judgments of right versus wrong. In these cases a member can honestly say to his constituents, "Tell me what you want." During my tenure with Congressman Santorum we labored to keep a Social Security office in a particular community because that town's leaders said it was important to them. We worked to keep certain public-housing developments restricted to elderly persons because hundreds of senior citizens demanded this; if local housing advocates had asked that these developments be opened to the homeless and no elderly residents objected, we would have taken the opposite position. Often the politician's job is to help people get what they want, not to tell them what they should or should not have.

Third, as we have already noted, legislators have to ration their attention among more competing priorities than they can possibly address. Most representatives will take the opportunity to get involved in a few issues of strong personal interest to them; for example, if I were in office, I would be active on adoption policy and religious-freedom issues whether these were hot items at the time or not. However, if they value their jobs, lawmakers will focus primarily on whatever issues the polls identify as of greatest concern to the voters.

Some people, usually those with a high level of ideological

motivation, are not comfortable with this responsibility. It irks them that candidates let polls tell them what issues to talk about. They wish that candidates could spend more time shaping and less time reflecting public sentiment. I respond by encouraging such persons to devote their energies to a special-interest lobbying organization or a think tank. A special-interest group can concentrate on whatever issues it chooses, and a think tank can promulgate bold, innovative policy statements without concern for political realities. These organizations, in order to survive, need to please not a majority of the voting public but only the far smaller constituency whose donations keep the doors open.

These roles are no less honorable than that of legislator; in fact, most groundbreaking policy initiatives originate in special-interest groups and think tanks, not with elected officials constrained by political realities. It is unreasonable, however, to expect a legislator whose job depends on public approval to follow the ideological priorities of a think tank.

The honest politician, then, can sincerely and justifiably tell constituents that he or she will take their views into consideration. One can actively offer voters one of the things they most want from their representatives: a listening ear, accompanied by a willingness to take up the people's concerns as his or her own. At the same time, politicians should circumscribe their flexibility with a clear inner awareness of the principles they will not sacrifice for electoral success. As a social conservative, I am fortunate that my wife's career brought me to Pittsburgh, where I fit in fairly well; but if we moved to San Francisco, I would abandon my political aspirations if necessary rather than revise my most deeply held views to mimic the surrounding culture.

Money
"How much money in campaign contributions did you receive from the American Trial Lawyers Association?" Any legislator who

votes against limiting multimillion-dollar punitive damages or medical malpractice awards can expect to face that question. For those who oppose gun control, it's "How much did the National Rifle Association pay for your vote?"

The assumption behind these attacks is that the representative's support is for sale to the highest bidder. Sometimes the assumption is right. In one of the more brazen cases, a Southern congressman allegedly told a wealthy woman who was lobbying for a particular tax incentive, "For $25,000 I can make it happen." The woman helped get the congressman knocked out of office, and he has since been indicted.

But usually the assumption is wrong, at least in its extreme form. Most legislators don't sell their vote to whoever offers them money; they determine their policies first and then appeal for support—financial and otherwise—from those who agree with those policies. They avoid dishonest money (i.e., bribes and illegal gifts) and treat honest money (i.e., campaign contributions) in the same way as the other forms of electoral influence we have already discussed. That is, willingness to contribute money, like willingness to staff a phone bank or generate constituent calls to the legislator's office, represents a measurement of the level of public concern. To the degree that the legislator can honestly (as discussed earlier in this chapter) let his constituency determine his actions, he can justifiably take these measurements into account when setting his priorities.

Does this mean our system of government permits rich people to have more influence than poor people? Absolutely. It also permits rich people to have more Cadillacs and more vacations, and nobody has proposed taxing the rich to provide bigger cars for the poor. In an ideal world, I might have it otherwise. But I submit that just as capitalism, though imperfect, remains distinctly preferable to socialism, so our present system of campaigns is, in principle, better than the alternatives.

Democratic elections cost money. Most members of Congress spent between $250,000 and $500,000 to win their last election. That money has to come from either the public purse (i.e., our taxes) or private pockets. Public financing of campaigns will not eliminate the need for private funding unless it is either extremely generous or tied to required limits on total spending; but such limits benefit incumbents by preventing challengers from raising the extra money they need in order to achieve name recognition.

There is respectful disagreement between honest, thoughtful persons on this issue, and turning to public financing could reduce the ability of extremely wealthy but poorly qualified candidates to buy victory by relying on their personal fortunes. But if we want meaningfully democratic elections, I think the best option is to let candidates raise as much money as they can and spend as much as they want. It is appropriate to limit the amount individuals or political-action committees (PACs) can give to a single campaign, and we could use some reforms to reduce the disproportionate role PACs currently play in campaign fundraising. But to try to take money out of politics creates, I believe, more problems than it solves.

Sometimes the most effective restraint on a legislator's behavior is not complex legal restrictions but the risk of disapproval by the electorate. A representative is free to take campaign contributions from the sugar industry and then vote for sugar subsidies at every opportunity; but if the Member has no sugar farmers in his district, a skillful challenger in the next election may be able to give the incumbent enough bad publicity, for taking money from a far-off special interest, to outweigh the value of the contribution.

What Money Can Buy
The honest politician can properly offer financial backers (or any other supporters) two benefits: access and priority. The value of

85

access results from the fact that, as we have noted, no legislator has the time to listen to everyone or to address every need. If I were a legislator, the constituent I met at my recent $500-a-person fundraiser would get a prompt meeting with me when he requested one.

At the staff level, access is not as prized a commodity, but *priority* is; all requests get answered, but the ones from key supporters get answered faster. As an aide I frequently dropped everything to give immediate attention to a "big hitter" (a person who had arranged a large fundraiser) or someone who had "maxed out" (i.e., given the maximum allowable campaign contribution) and who needed expeditious handling of government paperwork. I adopted this practice not because my boss asked me to do so (he never did), but because I considered it prudent. Even though, as I often assured less wealthy constituents, I never looked at our donation reports to see who had contributed, I usually knew when I was dealing with a big hitter. Either I already knew the person from crossing paths on the political scene, or the person had the presence of mind to call the campaign's fundraising staffer directly, who would in turn call me.

The real issue here in capturing the legislator's attention is not money but familiarity. The financial supporter becomes known to the representative, who is motivated to take a special interest in a personal friend; but the tireless campaign volunteer can achieve the same familiarity. So can the admirer who travels throughout the district to listen to every one of the legislator's presentations and offer unsolicited praise during the question period.

Note, however, that neither access nor priority presumes that big hitters or known supporters will get anything they wouldn't have received anyhow. Yes, they may get it faster, and that in itself may be a significant benefit. But a noncontributor who walked into the office with a three-day deadline for a visa approval would receive the same expediting. Yes, one can argue that access in some cases leads to advocacy, since we all tend to accept whichever side of an argument we hear most. But the ethical problems associated with the role of money in politics do not arise from advocacy on legitimate issues. Rather, ethical compromise results when a politician intervenes to seek personal benefits for friends, usually by interfering in the activities of a government agency. To avoid this pitfall, honest politicians must resolve never to seek for their friends anything of substantive value beyond what the merits of the case justify.

Most big hitters observe this limitation. In my experience, at least, I have found that they usually know what they can and cannot appropriately request and that, both for the sake of their own reputation and to protect the representative from public embarrassment, they draw the line in the right place. But perhaps my office's clean image made my experience artificially rosy by causing those less honorable to steer clear of me. After all, the media and prosecutors continue to uncover cases of political impropriety at all levels of government. And one friend who contemplated a run for state office told me that, when he contacted a few big hitters in search of initial financial commitments, some of them predicated their support on reciprocal commitments he considered unethical. But I have not generally found the prevalence of such behavior so great as to defy resistance.

To be thorough, I should mention a third category of honest favors contributors may receive. Along with access and priority, one can offer help in securing inherently political positions, such as leadership posts within the state governing body of one's political party. Just as wise legislators make political loyalty a prominent criterion in their hiring decisions, so they will seek to place committed supporters in key party offices or policy-making roles within their party's control. But those inherently political decisions are quite different from making politically motivated selections for nonpolitical positions, such as the slots each member of Congress is allotted at the U.S. Military Academy.

I'm So Important

Senator Mark Hatfield has pointed to the Senate elevators as an illustration of another political temptation: an inflated sense of self-importance. If a normal citizen enters the elevator at the lobby and pushes 3, but then a senator walks in and pushes the "Senators Only" button numbered 5, the elevator will bypass the third floor and go straight to the fifth floor. No wonder senators think the world revolves around them!

One would hope that regular church attendance, a reflective walk past a cemetery or a patient wait at the grocery store—where being a senator does not enable you to jump to the head of the line—would suffice to restore politicians to reality. But the higher politicians rise in stature, the busier they become, with less time for church, quiet walks or thoughtful reflection. They certainly don't do their own grocery shopping. They are pampered, flattered, praised, lobbied, wined and dined, chauffeured, flooded with VIP invitations and gifts, served by staff, featured in the media. Even the intensity of the criticism they face reminds them how important they have become. In Washington and many state capitals, the aura of power and self-importance sucks up staff along with the Members.

The solution to this problem is ultimately spiritual, as I will argue more forthrightly in chapter nine. But for now, let's settle for a few practical safeguards. Politicians can intentionally invite constructive criticism rather than lapping up fawning flattery from their staff and supporters. They can make themselves available regularly to the people they represent—not just in staged appearances but in extended visits and meetings where people have time to speak from their hearts and articulate their concerns. They can resolve each morning to act in such a way as to place their constituents' needs above their own. They can discipline themselves to fit inviolable family time in their schedules, as did Dan Quayle, who says he usually made it home for dinner while serving as vice president. And, of course, they can insist on doing their own grocery shopping.

The Bottom Line

We have discussed antidotes to several of the main temptations politicians face. Actually, though, for anyone with a conscience one antidote is enough: don't do anything that would make it harder for you to look in the mirror the next morning.

On most occasions another practical guideline is useful: don't do anything that would embarrass you if reported in the local newspaper. But sometimes, where the chance of exposure is minuscule, we must go beyond the threat of embarrassment and appeal directly to conscience.

I am firmly convinced that honesty and integrity are politically advantageous. I have heard too many citizens express their disgust with smooth politicians' evasive answers and their admiration for leaders who give straightforward, honest replies. It is the latter type of candidate who will inspire commitment and support from people who come to trust him or her—even if they do not share all of that person's views.

Sometimes, especially in the last heated weeks of a campaign, it may seem that dishonesty pays. The temptation to distort your opponent's record in your last damaging ads, knowing that the other side won't have time to strike back, can be great. So can the urge to distort your own record. Critics of former Oregon senator Bob Packwood claim him as the clearest recent illustration of that urge; they say he lied about his relationships with women, sneaking past election day before the truth could emerge and securing his Senate seat for another term until an ethics investigation forced his resignation. Those who want to serve honorably often feel that if they don't sling mud, distort the facts or make underhanded back-room compromises, they will simply pave the way to success for the opponent who has no similar scruples.

But before giving in to such thoughts, the honest politician will recall that there are higher goals than the next vote or the next election. Cheating may keep your candidate in office for another term, but it will also rob you of the sense of purpose that brought you to politics in the first place. It will enhance the cynicism and disillusionment that already cause too many good people to avoid politics, enlarging the power vacuum already too occupied by self-centered career-mongers consumed with their personal advancement.

The politician who has decided in advance what principles are nonnegotiable and who holds to that position, even under pressure—whose attitude toward possible defeat is a matter-of-fact "If I can't win honestly, I'll go do something else"—will always gain respect and will almost always gain influence in the long run.

6

ENJOYING
THE
PARTY

. . . .

So you're ready to do honest politics, until you realize that chapter five failed to address one big problem. To wield any influence in American politics you have to join one of the two major parties, both of which are crooked.

I understand how you feel that way. You've been watching the large number of straight party-line votes that occur at all levels of government, and you've become convinced that to succeed within either party one must discard independent thinking and do what the party boss says. You've seen top officeholders and party leaders campaign for all their own party's candidates, and you've said you could never bring yourself to believe all Democrats are good and all Republicans are bad, or vice versa.

Well, I think I have two pieces of good news for you. First, you don't have to join a party in order to be politically effective. But even better, joining a party isn't as awful as you may think. In this chapter we will see why not. But first, let's look at the pros and cons of the main alternatives.

Avoiding the Party

There are two main ways to be active outside party involvement. First, you can be a freelancer, as most of my friends have chosen to do. They become politically active when and if they feel like it, when a particular issue or a certain candidate of any party affiliation grabs their attention. This approach offers the greatest independence and the freedom to do only what you want, or to take a year off if you prefer. It also, although your involvement can still be valuable, offers the least potential for influence, because sporadic activity will not build a reputation, develop a following or earn any type of leadership position.

A second option is to channel your energy through an issue-focused organization rather than a political party. If you tend to identify a single issue or a small set of issues as the dominant factors that determine your opinion of a candidate, this option may be for you. Thousands of Americans focus their activism in this way, through the political activities of such organizations as the Christian Coalition, the National Organization for Women, the National Rifle Association, the Sierra Club, labor unions or chambers of commerce.

Single-issue advocates (especially if their issue is abortion or gun control) often get a bad rap from observers who consider it extreme, unbalanced and narrow-minded to focus exclusively on one issue when evaluating a candidate. I find this bad rap unjustified. Washington, D.C., and our state capitals swarm with thousands of paid single-issue advocates. We call them lobbyists, and they make a career of representing every special interest imaginable, from banks to textile producers to the homeless. (The

92

advocate for the homeless gets paid far less than those corporate lobbyists, but he is there nonetheless.) Though we may not admire all the tools of their trade, such as the lavish receptions and perks they offer in order to persuade elected officials and top aides to attend their functions, these people nevertheless play a necessary role in making sure the interest they represent is heard in the political process. If lobbyists do this as a career, why should private individuals who are so passionately committed to sportsmen's rights or environmental protection that this becomes the single issue of supreme importance to them not also be encouraged to follow their consciences? We may not agree with them, but we have no grounds to call their decisions less balanced or responsible than those of citizens who consider many issues roughly equal in importance.

Single-issue groups can wield significant power. In southwest Pennsylvania, a heavily Democratic but socially conservative region with a strong ethnic and religious base, prolifers are probably the most potent such organization. Their network can mobilize much-needed core volunteers in the early stages of a candidacy, and their lists of endorsed candidates gain wide distribution through churches and religious newspapers, swaying the estimated 5 to 10 percent of voters for whom this issue is decisive. As a result, prolife leaders are among the Pittsburgh area's most powerful grassroots political figures; prolife candidates energetically seek their help, and candidates who think they might be prolife ask these leaders to teach them how to be intelligently and convincingly prolife.

In other areas of the country, farmers, United We Stand (Ross Perot's organization), environmentalists or gay-rights activists may occupy a similar position of power. The last two groups, due to their tight networking and generally high level of political sophistication, often carry influence far beyond their numbers.

Single-issue activists frequently believe they can maintain

greater ideological purity in this way than if they affiliated with a political party. But unless they really do have an overwhelming commitment to their one issue, such may not be the case. One prolife leader told me she didn't like a certain incumbent's personal character or his stands on many other issues, "but we have to endorse him because he votes prolife." She was actually more boxed in than party members are, because she could not fail to endorse any prolife candidate without compromising her group's integrity as a single-issue organization.

Taking the Mystery Out of the Party

Being an active member of the local Republican party does not compel me to work for every Republican; I am only expected *not* to work for Democrats. In exchange for this voluntary commitment to limit my own freedom of speech, I obtain opportunities I could not have were I to remain outside the party structure. Most significantly, rather than simply deciding whether I like the candidates for local office, I get to help decide who those candidates will be.

I live in a community that, even though Republicans hold only a modest edge in the number of registered voters, has consistently elected a Republican-dominated school board. Although Republican candidates have to win a primary election first in order to get on the ballot for November, normally whoever gains the town Republican committee's endorsement gets with it the financial and community support needed to win. In other words, the membership of the school board in a town of over 30,000 people is largely determined by a few dozen active members of the town's Republican committee.

Before I joined the committee I never suspected that the process worked that way. Since then, through carefully chosen comments during endorsement debates, I believe I have had a direct impact on the complexion of my school board. Not that I deserve the primary credit for any particular results, or that all my other endeavors have been equally successful. But my friends who remain on the sidelines, declaring that neither major party is clean enough for them, miss this and many similar opportunities.

What does joining a party require you to do? Surprisingly little. In prior days, when party structures were stronger and party loyalty was more valued, party leaders could place greater demands on members. But in this age of individualism, parties are lucky to fill their committees at all, let alone fill them with good workers. If you are willing to distribute candidates' literature in your voting precinct, cover the polls on election day and occasionally give some extra help to a candidate you really like, your local Republican or Democratic committee will be pleased to have you. The more you build a reputation as a knowledgeable spokesperson or hard worker, the more weight your voice will carry. But the minimum requirement is indeed quite minimal.

The place to start is the party committee in your own municipality. It probably meets periodically, perhaps once a month, to discuss issues of local concern, hear from candidates and plan its political activities. Depending on your local rules, you may need to place your name on a formal ballot for election as a party committee member, or the party chairperson may simply appoint you to a vacancy. The committee should then invite you to an orientation session where you learn about procedures and responsibilities (many of which will be familiar to you if you have read this book carefully).

Just by virtue of your committee membership you can expect to become more "in the loop" than you were previously. Local elected officials from your party will put you on their mailing lists and invite you to their picnics. Candidates for office, long before they publicly announce their plans, will come to your meetings or call you personally, seeking commitments of support. No longer will you have trouble finding out what they believe; instead you'll have ample opportunity to question them. Did you ever wonder who dropped that campaign literature in your door the weekend before election day? Now you'll be asked to serve as that person for your precinct.

At this point you will begin to position yourself within the party. The path of least resistance is to help all candidates, but that path may prevent you from giving substantial help to any of them. As you interact with fellow committee members, you will probably discover that many of them don't support all the party's nominated candidates. In fact, they may not even like all the candidates. In addition to the inevitable personal dislikes and personality conflicts, chances are good that your local committee reflects the same intraparty divisions about which you read in news articles on state or national government.

The differences will show up most clearly in contested primary elections—when the committee is not generating support for its candidates but trying to decide who those candidates will be— and perhaps also in elections of the committee's own officers. Some committee members may consistently get gung-ho for those hopefuls who show particular vigor for cutting taxes, while others never seem to lift a finger for anyone who supports gun controls. (The latter is a case of the single-issue activist transformed into a one-issue litmus-test party member, working within the party structure to promote candidates who hold the right view on their key issue. Issue-based organizations try to advance their cause by placing such persons inside both parties.)

Hopefully you and your colleagues will manage to handle with civility whatever disagreements may arise; politics needs respectful people who can express their disagreements frankly without becoming disagreeable. But don't expect to be forced into rigid party-line conformity. Even when the party committee formally votes to endorse certain candidates in a contested primary, party leaders seldom try to silence members who stick with unen-

96

dorsed candidates. They know they can't afford to alienate good party members who will usually be their allies, and besides, heavy-handed attempts to silence party regulars' right to dissent tend to backfire on the perpetrator.

The dynamics change in times of intense intraparty rivalry between opposing factions, as in the numerous recent instances where proponents and detractors of the Christian Right have clashed over control of local and state Republican party committees. On such occasions you may feel unpleasantly pressured to take sides and distrusted by both sides if you refuse to choose. (Or perhaps your main reason for joining the party is to strengthen your side in a conflict like this one.) But in less contentious circumstances, the only obligation you may find it difficult to avoid will probably be the task of passing out "slate cards" promoting your party's whole slate of candidates at election time. Beyond that, if you show support for those candidates whom you like, you will earn tacit permission to steer clear of those who don't excite you.

Except in those areas where the party "machine" remains strong, the real pressure toward party loyalty occurs not when you first join the committee but if you seek party leadership, and it comes not through indoctrination so much as from the nature of the job to which you aspire. Even a party-endorsed candidate or public officeholder can speak for himself or herself, and sometimes one does so quite boldly. In 1994, Virginia's Republican senator denounced fellow Republican Oliver North's bid to join him in the Senate, while Pennsylvania's Democratic governor refused to support his own lieutenant governor's effort to succeed him—even after these candidates won their party's nominations. On the other hand, a *party* officeholder (e.g., a local committee chairperson) speaks on behalf of the party and thus has a greater obligation to be publicly supportive of all its candidates.

Here, as at the initial point of entering the party, there are tradeoffs. In exchange for a commitment to speak favorably of all the party's candidates and activities, a party official gains a greater role in setting that party's direction and determining how its resources will be used. The party leader retains latitude for personal preference, but simply has to express it differently. Whereas the rank-and-file party member may decline to support some candidates, the party official agrees to endorse them, but exhibits less enthusiasm for them than for his or her favorites.

They're Not Just Hacks

If this cursory description of political party activity doesn't enthrall you, fine. But I hope you will at least concede that Republican or Democratic leaders need not be mindless political hacks blindly deceiving themselves that everything their party does is good. Not only do they maintain the freedom to communicate their individual preferences, but theirs is nothing more than a common situation paralleled throughout our society. After all, when did you last hear IBM's public-affairs office criticize IBM, or your university's alumni-relations director attack the college?

It should be noted, though, that the political process in our two-party system contains additional incentives that encourage party loyalty. One receives opportunities for advancement in one's party by pleasing its leaders, who themselves, in most cases, have sought and attained these positions because of their broad commitment to that party's interests. In legislative bodies, each party's leadership controls many of the benefits—committee assignments, staff allotments, chances to make public speeches on the party's behalf—for which legislators yearn. The Member loyal to his or her party leadership stands to reap rewards, while the renegade can expect a cold shoulder.

Paradoxically, party leaders can generally exert the least control over their most vulnerable legislators, those whose seats could be most easily lost to the other party. Near-complete loyalty can be demanded of a Democratic lawmaker in an overwhelmingly Democratic urban district, but a Democrat representing a Republican-leaning suburban area must be permitted to side with his or her constituency and against the party in order to remain electable.

President Clinton's 1993 budget plan (the one Republicans would call "the largest tax increase in American history") left us a graphic illustration of this principle. When it passed the House of Representatives without a vote to spare, the last Member persuaded to support it was Congresswoman Marjorie Margolies-Mezvinsky, a first-term Democrat representing an affluent, heavily Republican district outside Philadelphia. Clinton won the day, but Margolies-Mezvinsky's "courageous vote" and her loyalty to her party's leader lost the Democrats a House seat the following year, as she could not overcome this perceived soak-the-rich tax vote to win reelection despite spending $1.6 million on her campaign. Democrats must wish, in retrospect, that they could have let her save her courage for another occasion. Similarly, a Republican from an urban area can get away with bucking the party and advocating state and federal spending to help cities much more easily than a suburban member can.

Most legislators, though, have good reason to vote predominantly with their own party. They also have good cause to work for the election of more members of their party, regardless of those prospective colleagues' views. For the clearest reason why, consider what happens when the minority party in a legislature becomes the majority. Suddenly they double their staff complement, chair all the committees, set the legislative agenda and determine the rules of debate. Having more members of your party in office greatly increases your ability to accomplish your legislative and political goals.

Another reason for party-line voting is that the two parties really do see things differently. Almost all elected officials have consciously aligned themselves with the party with which they have closer ideological affinity. Thus it should not be surprising that, on issues that sharply divide the two parties, votes will closely follow party lines.

What the Parties Stand For

If you've decided that maybe joining a party isn't such a bad idea after all, perhaps your next question is *which* party to join. Gosh, I thought you'd never ask. But since I've already revealed my preference back in chapter one, I'll try to stay nonpartisan here and give a balanced sketch of the core values for which each party stands.

The head of a leading antitax organization once told me, "The essential issue that separates the parties is taxes." That's only half the story—the Republican half. If that were the whole story, the Republicans would win the popularity battle hands down. Nobody likes paying taxes, but most people recognize that the government that collects more taxes can also provide more services.

The crucial question distinguishing the parties is not "How much should we tax?" but "What is government's role?" Republicans tend to believe in limiting the role of government and giving greater freedom and responsibility to individuals, families and private organizations. Democrats tend to believe in a larger role for government in guaranteeing opportunity for all persons and in establishing the terms of the good society.

This basic disagreement over whether government is primarily a promoter of good or a restrainer of evil defines the divergence between the parties on most of today's major issues. Republicans have generally supported lower taxes, a stronger national defense, cuts in social programs, parental choice in education, free-market economics, private property rights and tough punishment of criminals. In contrast, Democrats have been more willing to support reduced defense spending, expanded social programs, public education, labor rights, affirmative action, environmental protection, greater redistribution of income to assist the needy, and rehabilitation of criminals. The consistent theme in all these debates is that Democrats lean toward using the power of government to improve society, while Republicans prefer (except in cases of public safety and national security) to improve society by getting government out of the way as much as possible.

In addition, on matters of social policy, those wishing to restrict abortion and gay rights predominate in the Republican party while those tolerant of such practices have gravitated toward the Democratic party. Whether this divergence follows logically from the two parties' philosophical foundations or represents a quirk of American politics is a discussion for another book.

The differences I have here tried to enumerate fairly and dispassionately serve as the basis for most of the considerably more passionate rhetoric observed in partisan debates. When wearing my Republican hat, I perceive clearly that Democrats are tax-and-spend liberals who coddle criminals, confiscate my hard-earned money to fund government jobs for loyal Democratic social workers, burden the small businessman with endless regulations in the name of social engineering, and show more concern for spotted owls and wetlands than for people's jobs. My Democratic friends, meanwhile, know me as a heartless capitalist who would gut the public schools, permit businesses to take advantage of their workers, and let the unemployed and disabled go homeless so that wealthy Republicans can drive BMWs and sip cocktails at the country club. Between campaigns, however, we recognize each other as esteemed colleagues with valuable ideas and justifiable concerns, all of which must be balanced as we seek to reach a governing consensus and implement responsible public policies.

Each party encompasses a broad range of views, and neither party can hope for uniformity on any issue. But politicians generally choose to join the party with which they agree more often. There is, of course, considerable overlap in the middle, further complicated by regional variations, the most significant of which is the predominance of conservative Democrats in the southern states. But the cynic who growls "There's no difference between the parties" is documentably wrong.

Not everyone considers ideology at all in choosing a party. Some feel bound by family tradition. Others become active with the party in power in hopes of landing a government job. In the heavily Democratic areas around Pittsburgh, community leaders with thoroughly Republican philosophies register as Democrats because they could not win election to local office as Republicans. Fascinatingly, in many of these communities, two identifiable factions emerge; the only differences from the normal two-party system are that here both "parties" are registered as Democrats and they fight their battles in the primary rather than the general election.

For those who intend their political activism to be independent of party structures, party registration matters little, except in those states where one can vote only in the primary elections of one's own party. However, one who wishes to work within a party should usually affiliate with the one closest to his or her own views, lest one become marginalized or ineffective due to unwillingness to support many of that party's candidates. As one progresses in politics it becomes harder to jump parties—but never impossible: during 1995 the elite 100-member U.S. Senate contained no fewer than four men who had switched parties after entering Congress.

More Parties
I have saved for last the option of joining a party other than the major two. If you seek a party more to your liking than either Republicans or Democrats, you have plenty of other choices:

102

Reform Party, New Party, Patriots, Libertarians, Taxpayers Alliance, Socialists and more, not to mention independent candidates running for office with no party affiliation. Minor parties tend to hover quietly around the fringes, if they survive at all. Not one of them has become a significant factor in American politics since the Republicans established themselves as the second major party in 1860.

But before you abandon this option, consider the impact minor parties and independents do have. They almost never win—though in recent years well-known independents have won statewide races in Alaska, Connecticut and Vermont—but they often affect the outcome.

In the short run, they may appear to do so in counterproductive ways, since they tend to suck votes away from the major-party candidate ideologically closer to them, often creating the margin of victory for the other, still less desirable major candidate. But this devilish potential to sabotage a major party's campaign is exactly the source of the minor party's power. Persons who can credibly threaten to wage a third-party campaign can negotiate valuable concessions from the major-party candidate who knows the 5 percent or even 2 percent of the votes likely to be siphoned off could decide the winner. (Ross Perot, before forming his own party, mastered this strategy through his United We Stand America organization, to the extent that Republican presidential candidates paid more attention to him than to virtually any Republican.) The independent is negotiating from strength if the major-party candidate is desperate to persuade him or her to stay out of the race. If you choose the independent or minor-party path and pursue it successfully, you will gain influence within the major party closer to you—as a troublesome rebel, but one who must be kept satisfied.

New York is one state where minor parties have solidified a modicum of influence, taking advantage of election laws that permit candidates to be listed in more than one row on the ballot. In this way the Conservative and Liberal parties can nominate their own full slate of candidates, even if their slate mirrors that of one of the major parties. Usually the Conservatives and Liberals agree to go along with the Republican and Democratic nominations (respectively), but they reserve the right to deviate from the major party's line if the Republican candidate is insufficiently conservative or the Democrat not liberal enough. Their ability to deliver a serious blow to a major-party candidate helps to ensure that their voice is heard.

Even if you have little hope of winning or affecting the outcome, declaring a candidacy provides a wonderful forum to present ideas to the public. Stand outside the grocery shouting "Government is crooked!" and you'll become known as the local goofball, but get on the ballot as an independent candidate for governor and you may get equal exposure with the major candidates in statewide debates. In many states a couple dozen committed door-knockers can obtain the required number of petition signatures to qualify their candidate for a spot on the ballot.

Americans frustrated with two-party domination often point out that our system discourages the creation of new parties. Many other countries fill their legislatures not by winner-takes-all elections (in which the top vote getter wins the race and the others get nothing) but by proportional representation, according to which each party is awarded a number of seats proportional to its percentage of the total vote. Under this system, for example, Libertarians or Socialists could, by garnering just 2 percent of the vote in California, earn one of that state's more than 50 seats in the U.S. House.

Israel has shown the impact of proportional seating on those occasions when its national elections left neither major party holding a majority in its parliament. As a result, tiny "ultrareligious" parties that would have no seats under an American-style system held the balance of power, possessing the ability to make either party the governing majority (if they chose to cooperate with that party) or to block virtually all legislation by siding with neither.

You may not like the American bias toward a two-party system. But perhaps it will be some consolation to know that, whatever your views, there is almost certainly room for you in at least one of the major parties should you find that route attractive. California may not have any Libertarians or Socialists (at least, not with a capital L or S) in its state legislature, but it has everything from unreconstructed liberals from Berkeley or inner-city Los Angeles to archconservatives from Orange County. You should not expect to find everything about party membership or about any system of government agreeable; as I frequently observe with a shrug, there is no perfect justice this side of heaven. But neither should you expect to find party activism incompatible with honest politics.

7

GETTING
YOUR FACTS
STRAIGHT

. . . .

Whenever people say they trust what they learn from the media, I tell them about my congressman's appearance in the *New Yorker* literary magazine.

One day a constituent called Congressman Santorum's office to complain about a lost manuscript. He had submitted an unsolicited composition several months earlier to the *New Yorker*. He had never received a reply and wondered if an inquiry from the congressman would help.

I told the caller that, since the *New Yorker* did not receive federal funding, I doubted that we would have any more influence than he, but that if he put the facts of the matter in writing I would make a courtesy call for him. He did so, and I phoned the *New Yorker*—with a good-natured disclaimer that "we sure do get all kinds of inquiries at a congressional office." The staff member there explained that their turnaround time was about six weeks, so anything sent three months ago must have been lost. I passed the bad news along to the constituent.

A few days later Congressman Santorum received a call from the *New Yorker* staff. They thought the story of a congressman trying to track down a lost manuscript merited a brief mention in their next issue. Santorum offered a few comments to the caller, who assured him that we'd like the final version.

Here (from its February 3, 1992, edition) is the full text of what resulted when the *New Yorker* staff applied its creativity to this episode:

> The other day, the phone rang and a voice that sounded distinctly like a voice of the people asked, "Is this *The New Yorker?*"
>
> "Yes, it is," we said.
>
> "This is Rick Santorum's office," the voice said. "Congressman Rick Santorum, of the Eighteenth Congressional District, in suburban Pittsburgh. One of our constituents asked that we look into the whereabouts of a manuscript he sent you, in good faith, for your perusal. He hasn't heard from you in some time, and would like to have his manuscript returned to him now, please."
>
> We explained that this magazine receives about a thousand unsolicited manuscripts a week, or fifty thousand a year. We try to respond quickly, but sometimes the mails swallow an envelope, or a manuscript mysteriously files itself behind a desk. Usually, it resurfaces sooner or later.
>
> The voice said that it would report back to the angry constituent, and added, "In all likelihood, you'll hear from me again."
>
> We were chastened, but only for a minute. Then we felt flattered, uplifted, patriotic. For the first time in our history,

perhaps in all literary history, the United States Government had come to the aid of an anxious author—a member of a downtrodden minority, if ever there was one. At a time when term-limit propositions are turning up on many ballots, and when public confidence in our elected officials may be drooping to an all-time low, we had just found a politician to cheer for. We support Rep. Santorum (R., Pa.) to the hilt. We support him for senator in 1992. We support him for President in 1996. Vote Santorum!

Santorum did indeed enjoy the story. He faxed copies all over the place, including one to Arlen Specter, then a candidate for re-election as a U.S. senator from Pennsylvania, with a cover note reading, "Don't worry, I'm not running."

It was all a good laugh until a hard-nosed Associated Press reporter picked up the scent. Apparently taking the New Yorker's colorful rendition as factually accurate, he called Santorum and questioned him on why taxpayer resources were used in pursuit of a lost manuscript. (No matter that the resources expended totaled one very short phone call and one piece of mail.) By the time this reporter had finished, the original article's creative license had been transformed into a serious journalistic report implying that our office really did pressure the New Yorker. The Associated Press article even named me, as befits the cardinal rule of political loyalty: when something good happens, credit the Member, but when things turn sour, blame the aide.

A local newspaper not only gave the story front-page attention but followed up with an editorial two days later, criticizing this style of constituent service. For weeks I answered every phone call fearing that the caller would say, "Are you the guy who thinks the New Yorker is a federal agency?"

Somehow my political career survived this incident, but the episode remains a classic example of how the media can mislead as well as inform. To do honest politics you must avoid overly naive reliance on the media. But this raises a more difficult question: how *do* you get reliable information?

Understanding the Media

First, since the media will remain your primary source of information, let's look at what the media are and what they are not.

The media are not neutral. In some cases that's obvious because they openly promote their preferences. *Mother Jones* magazine has a liberal agenda, the *American Spectator* a conservative agenda. Accordingly, each one presents only its own side of the argument. Newspaper editorial boards and talk-show hosts use their positions as a platform from which to spread their views.

What we forget is that, since we all have personal opinions, no one can be purely objective. The media figures who do not parade their personal biases still have them, more subtle—perhaps even unconscious—and thus harder to detect. A reporter sympathetic to gay concerns may depict AIDS activists kindly and question their opponents relentlessly, while a colleague with a different bias might focus on the transfer to AIDS research of money that could otherwise have been used to fight cancer. Neither one is consciously skewing the report, yet their own views have colored how they frame the story. Even if they do not express their own opinions, the sources they choose to interview, questions they ask and clips they select can greatly alter the report's public impact.

Even the question of what is newsworthy defies attempts to claim neutrality. Studies have shown the media to be more liberal, both politically and morally, and less religious than the general public. Thus many media sources may pay relatively scant attention to the role of religion in society, since they do not see religion playing a role in their own world. Social conflict and political change make news, so religion and other aspects of culture are not newsworthy unless they provoke conflict.

The media are entertainers. They're not broadcasting or writing as a favor to you. Most media sources are for-profit corporations, and even publicly funded stations keenly watch the ratings. To survive they must maximize the number of users, and to attract an audience they must entertain, not just inform. Thoughtful, in-depth reporting can find a niche, as evidenced by the *Wall Street Journal* with its lengthy stories, total lack of photographs, unchanging visual presentation and loyal readership. But the masses, with their thirty-second attention span, have turned to television and its thirty-second, visually grabbing news stories.

The need to entertain not only limits the depth of reporting but affects its content. Angry conservatives who assailed the "liberal media" for their attacks on Presidents Reagan and Bush should have discovered by now that the media are, for the most part, equal-opportunity devourers. Controversy sells, so they attack everybody. Gossip sells, so they dig up and expose private dirt.

The media have limited time and space. An evening TV newscast presents about as much information as two pages of a daily newspaper. Newspapers can cover more items, but still often in only very sketchy fashion.

A Pittsburgh newspaper once printed a listing of area congressmen's votes on a proposal to reduce funding for the National Endowment for the Arts by 2 percent. From the skeletal description of the proposal, those voting no would have appeared to be staunch backers of arts funding. Readers with no other source of information on the debate would never have suspected that many of the opponents voted no to protest their inability to propose a *larger* cut.

For those wanting to follow the political process closely, the mass media are not only too limited but too late in their coverage. By the time these sources tell you about a pending legislative proposal, that bill has probably moved through hear-

111

ings, out of committee and within a few days of consideration by the full House or Senate. The point where you could have had the greatest impact on the process may have passed months ago.

The media can be duped. The subjects of media coverage often seek to manipulate the media so as to cast themselves in a favorable light. Politicians have a distinct interest in taking credit for good news whether they deserve it or not, fooling unsophisticated and gullible reporters along the way if possible.

For example, legislators often deserve no credit for grants awarded to organizations in their district, but they don't want you to know that when they announce the award. One school principal told me that, when the West Virginia school he had previously administered won an excellence award from the U.S. Education Department, he learned about it from the local media—because the local congressman, upon receiving advance notice of the award, notified the media and not the school. (Had I been the reporter, I might have indulged my own bias by writing a story on the congressman's appalling chutzpah.)

The media are usually fair. Despite their humanness, their personal biases, and the tight deadlines that sometimes cause them to confuse facts or miss nuances of a story, the media generally try to be fair and, in my opinion, usually succeed. Our increasingly impatient and shallow society's demand for entertainment may be driving the media, more than in earlier times, to make news rather than simply deliver it, fully justifying the continued existence of watchdog groups that pounce on alleged media abuses. My wife knows how often I, as a critical viewer, have shouted angrily at the television in the midst of a network news segment, "That's advocacy journalism!" But for the most part, good journalistic ethics prevails: whatever else they do with a story, they still want to get the facts right and the opinions balanced.

112

Beware of the Tricksters

Not so with professional political consultants, paid to persuade—if not mislead—the public by crafting a likable image of their own candidate while trashing the opponent. Their job is not to educate but to win. Accordingly, their assignment drives them to judge prospective appeals not by whether they are accurate but by whether the approach will backfire when the opponent strikes back.

Frustrated observers and participants alike have called for greater accountability in political advertising—but to whom? In recent years the media have improved the situation by critically examining the factual claims made in political ads, thus increasing the risk campaigns run if they try to publish distortions. Still, however, far more voters see the ads than read or hear the analyses, leaving many campaigns little motivated to worry about truth, especially in those last hectic days when the other side no longer has time to refute inaccuracies.

My prime firsthand experience of this sort became a national news story. During the 1994 U.S. Senate campaign in Pennsylvania, Rick Santorum told an audience of college students that, in order to keep the Social Security system solvent, he favored gradually increasing the eligibility age for benefits by one month per year until it reached age seventy, or perhaps even higher. A campaign staffer for his opponent, Harris Wofford, videotaped the event. Two weeks before election day the Wofford campaign released a television ad that skillfully spliced excerpts of Santorum's remarks with a narrator's comment, "Rick Santorum wants to delay social security until you're seventy," so as to leave the impression that Santorum wanted to raise the age to seventy immediately, for all recipients, regardless of the amount they had paid into the system.

The ad was a killer, mainly because it gave the appearance of credulity by showing Santorum himself speaking. Wofford eliminated a ten-point deficit in the polls in a matter of days. One voter, told by a reporter that Santorum's comments had been pulled out of context, replied, "How could they be out of context? They're his own words." (I wished I could have asked that simpleton whose words he expected the Wofford campaign to pull out of context!) Had Santorum not had two weeks (I presume the Wofford campaign would have waited one more week to release the ad had their candidate been staying closer in the polls) and plenty of cash to respond to the attack, Wofford would have emerged victorious.

The tactic also unleashed bitter controversy, with one Pittsburgh columnist editorializing after election day about Wofford's attempt to use the "Big Lie" to seize victory. My point is not to claim that either side was spotless in this furiously contested race, though I do feel this Wofford ad went beyond generally accepted standards of selective presentation in political advertising. Rather, the point is that, if the Santorum campaign does not like a Wofford ad, it is the Santorum campaign's job, and nobody else's, to refute or anticipate it. That's what democratic elections are all about. Much as in court, each side presents its own case as persuasively as possible, with the voters functioning as judge. Nobody ever promised that the democratic process would elect the wiser or more honorable candidate. Short of the threat of lawsuits and ethics investigations should a campaign engage in libel or other criminal activity, the best precaution against dishonorable campaigning is an informed, attentive electorate.

Distortions aside, the negative advertising that dominates most hard-fought races has received such widespread criticism that one would think everyone hates it. If that were the case, of course, no one would use negative ads.

To the contrary, although a candidate with nothing positive to say will alienate the voters, attack ads are more widely noticed and have more powerful impact than strictly positive appeals and are thus indispensable in high-profile contests.

In response to those who deplore negative campaigning, I would argue that as long as it does not engage in blatant distortion, it is perfectly legitimate. The basic task of any campaign is to make the voters choose that candidate (or, in a referendum, that position) as the best available option. There is no reason why the campaign should not share, along with good things about its own candidate, unattractive information about the other candidates as part of its effort to achieve that goal. Given the virtual necessity of negative campaigning to get the attention of a large chunk of the electorate, you should not disparage candidates who feel compelled to use it.

Getting Better Information

The charges and countercharges always flying in politics do make it all the more difficult to figure out who's telling the truth and who really stands for what. Now that we've seen the challenges, let's look at some solutions to the information problem.

With regard to Congress, there's no lack of information, if you have the time. You can get the unadulterated version of Congress by watching C-SPAN, which televises the House and Senate in live session and serves an extraordinary menu of informative programming at other times. If your spouse fears that you'll become a C-SPAN junkie and terminates your cable subscription, hit the best library in town and see if it subscribes to *Congressional Quarterly*, actually a weekly magazine that covers Congress thoroughly and lists every vote cast by every Member. Don't plan on getting a home subscription, though, as the cost exceeds $1000 per year. Even *Roll Call*, the twice-weekly newspaper devoted to happenings on Capitol Hill, costs several hundred dollars for a one-year subscription. You may be able to access similar publications on activities in your own state, though if so you can count on finding these low-circulation items similarly expensive.

115

The rapid expansion of on-line computer information is delivering new solutions to the problems of minimal information access and high costs. But if your interests lie mainly within one or two definable issue areas, there is a much less costly remedy: hook up with an organization devoted to those concerns. For a small subscription fee or donation, you can receive that group's newsletter or periodic updates designed to keep you abreast of relevant legislative developments and to advise you of recommended actions, such as contacting your legislators to urge support for a certain bill. The organization may also send you information on the positions each candidate for office has taken or scorecards rating current lawmakers' voting records. It may even have a fax network for those times when quick action is needed.

In making use of issue-focused organizations, however, make sure you know their agenda. Yes, they too, like politicians and the media, have an agenda of their own, and it may not always parallel yours. For example, the Sierra Club is a highly recommended information source on environmental issues, but that does not mean everyone concerned about environmental conservation shares the Sierra Club's position on population control. Moreover, despite frequent protestations to the contrary, politically active issue groups are notorious for skewing their scorecards, carefully selecting the votes cited so as to exaggerate the difference between the preferred candidate and the opponent.

There I go again, making the process of information-gathering seem hopelessly complicated, right? Well, don't despair too much. But you will want to evaluate all information sources with a critical eye and to remember there are at least two sides to every story. One of the best ways to gauge the reliability of the information you receive is to behave like a good journalist: call the other side and ask for comment.

If your realtors' association newsletter tells you Senator Jackson has consistently voted against the interests of realtors, ask Jackson's office if they can give any reasons why realtors should view Jackson more favorably. If the aide is speechless, consider the newsletter confirmed; if the aide provides you with a response, you now have two perspectives to evaluate in determining where you line up. You can always go back to the realtors' association for more details if Jackson is disputing their facts.

If an opponent's attack ad raises doubts about a candidate you like, call the candidate's campaign office and ask for their refutation. If you want to know where a candidate stands on the issues, request his or her issue papers. So few citizens interact with campaigns in this way that you will usually have little trouble getting attention. Campaigns assume that voters who make the effort to get informed are probably also strategic voters who influence their friends and neighbors.

This type of direct inquiry is especially valuable in local races that receive little news coverage, such as for district judge or town council. In these contests the problem is not sorting out false claims but getting any information at all; debates are seldom scheduled, since hardly anyone would attend, and a candidate or officeholder may receive just two sincerely inquisitive calls like yours in a month (and may thus find the chance to discuss issues with you enjoyable rather than bothersome).

As you develop the practice of withholding judgment until you've checked the other side of the story—a valuable habit for all of life, not just politics—you may find yourself beginning to counterargue. Instinctively, as you read a news report or listen to a campaign ad, ideas of what the other side might be will form in your mind. This discipline will make you a wiser consumer of everything you read and hear, including the mass media. You will not be as quickly persuaded by outside opinions like newspaper endorsements without first considering what policy biases or philosophical presuppositions motivated the opinions and whether you share those often unstated yet crucial foundations.

117

I recall watching a national news report, during the 1992 presidential campaign, that compared George Bush's and Bill Clinton's proposals for education. In the three minutes allotted, the reporter described the two candidates' positions in terms of how much federal funding each one advocated for various education programs. I immediately spotted the implicit presupposition that spending more federal money makes better education—an assumption I consider questionable—and evaluated the information presented accordingly.

None of us can totally avoid consuming erroneous or distorted information. However, developing a critical perspective not only gives you the confidence to overcome that helpless "I don't know whom to believe" feeling but also strengthens your ability to present your thoughts to others in a rigorous, convincing fashion.

Your Turn to Manipulate

Having laid bare the ways in which information sources can manipulate you, let's turn the tables and offer a few tips on how you can win more favorable treatment from the media for yourself or your cause.

Be in touch. Many interests, political and otherwise, get no media attention because they ask for none. Your campaign or any other concern should visit all the local media outlets, build personal contacts, keep them regularly apprised of your activities and make follow-up calls when you really want coverage.

Be cordial. With the exception of the rare adversarial reporter, you will seldom gain by refusing to cooperate with the media when you are their subject. Go the extra mile to help them get information for a story, and they'll be less inclined to bash you. That doesn't mean you have to answer all their questions, but you can be cordial even when declining to comment.

Be professional. Give media sources a good product. Press releases should be well composed, written in journalistic style (e.g.,

118

sharp, straightforward sentences, with the key facts plainly communicated right at the top), in a format resembling what the media are accustomed to seeing. If you do a good job, smaller newspapers looking to fill space without working too hard may print your release verbatim.

Be available. Make sure that a designated, capable representative (press secretary or public-relations staffer) is available to the media at all times. You don't want to miss an opportunity because the reporter couldn't find you for comment before a deadline.

Be strategic. Identify the two or three points you want reported and keep restating them. The more often you emphasize your key points in an interview, the more likely they are to show up in the story (and the fewer alternative comments you serve up as fodder for a reporter who might wish to spin the story in a different direction). Watch skillful politicians being interviewed, and see how they return to the points they want to drive home, no matter what the question is, and so smoothly that you never notice they are dodging the question. Remember also that you don't have to answer every question you're asked, nor do you need to comment at all if you don't believe it is in your interest to do so at the time.

Be entertaining. Since the media want to entertain, you'll get more coverage if you help them do so. If you want your press conference to make the local television news, provide a colorful visual display, not just a talking head. Deliver your main points with memorable one-liners, and the news reports on that meeting will quote your catchy "sound bite."

Again, sharp politicians work hard to make their key lines irresistible to the media. In one Senate committee hearing on President Clinton's health care reform proposal, with the cameras rolling, Utah Republican Orrin Hatch let loose with a criticism so cutting and colorfully worded that Democrat Ted Kennedy interrupted with a chuckle, "Is that the sound bite for this evening's news?" It was, of course. I saw it on two networks that evening.

119

Keep watch. Monitor the coverage the media give you. If you feel you have been unfairly treated, let the reporter and manager know. You may wish to request a correction or time to respond. If a media source knows that you and your followers won't tolerate slanted coverage without speaking up, it is less likely to risk offending you.

8

THE PHYSIQUE
OF A
POLITICIAN

. . . .

I don't know if I'll run for another term," Pam lamented. "I'm not sure I can last that long."

I had taken Pam to lunch because I knew she needed the encouragement. She was an active, widely appreciated parent in her school district who had reluctantly accepted an invitation to run for school board. She had won and was now in the third year of a four-year term.

Pam had served well, but at great emotional cost. The level of mudslinging between two opposing factions far surpassed typical political rhetoric and even degenerated into lawsuits. The opposing faction had vilified several of her allies in the last election, defeating two of them and leaving Pam and her remaining friends as a minority on the board; from then on Pam could do little more than object as the majority faction consistently outvoted her. There are two sides to every story, as we now know, but to most observers many of the new majority's actions seemed more intended to exact revenge on political foes (like the soccer coach, who had campaigned for Pam's friends and was fired without explanation) than to benefit the school district.

Pam, an accomplished painter and inexperienced politician, was caught in the midst of all this. She wanted to upgrade her school district's arts program, not engage in angry debates and vicious campaigns. The experience had not been what she expected, and she didn't want to deal with it any longer.

The political atmosphere of Pam's school board was far more charged than most. Chances are that you won't have it as bad. But then again, you might. Better to know what you're getting into, including the risks, than to be unprepared for the unpleasant experiences that may await you. Best of all is to identify and develop the skills you will need in order to perform the role you envision for yourself. This chapter should help you decide what parts of your "physique" need attention and where you are already strong.

Thick Skin

In addition to praising Pam's grace and patience and buying her lunch, I shared with her one of my most common admonitions: don't get into politics at any level if you don't have a thick skin.

I remember how frustrated Rick Santorum's wife became when some of his yard signs disappeared during his first campaign. She wanted to call the media and expose the evil deeds she attributed to the opponent's dishonorable style of campaigning. Since then I've participated in many more campaigns, and every one has been spiced with charges of stolen signs—on both sides. Even politicians who decry such activity cannot always fully control the zeal of their supporters.

The Physique of a Politician

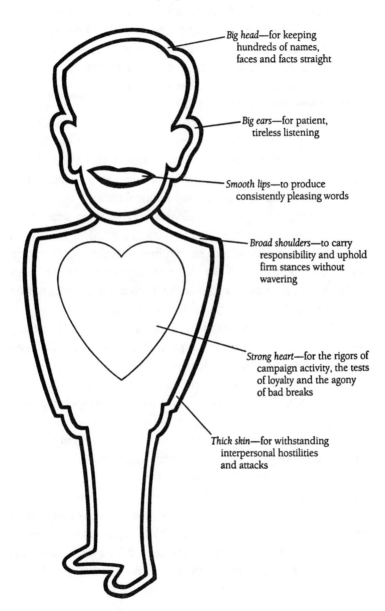

Big head—for keeping hundreds of names, faces and facts straight

Big ears—for patient, tireless listening

Smooth lips—to produce consistently pleasing words

Broad shoulders—to carry responsibility and uphold firm stances without wavering

Strong heart—for the rigors of campaign activity, the tests of loyalty and the agony of bad breaks

Thick skin—for withstanding interpersonal hostilities and attacks

123

In any tough race you can count on your candidate being splattered with mud. Each candidate seeks to spotlight selectively the most embarrassing, unpopular aspects of the opponent's record. Along the way selective presentation often shades into distortion, and distortions degenerate into outright lies. At least that's how each side sees the other side's behavior.

Less scrupulous strategists won't even stop to ask "Is it true?" about their contemplated attacks, but simply "Will it stick?" If it will bring net benefit to their candidate, they will use it. You might just as fruitfully clamor for justice against those goon hockey players who injure the opposing star when the officials' backs are turned as try to stop these dirty political tricks.

You'd better develop your thick skin so that these attacks will neither disillusion you nor goad you into responding in kind or without restraint. A politician should never display anger, except in a premeditated fashion calculated to improve his or her image (as when President Bush blasted CBS anchorman Dan Rather on the evening news so as to dispel his "wimp" label).

You'll need your thick skin not only at election time but any time your government body or party committee—or whatever group you are involved in—deliberates. Working in a congressman's district office, I soon learned that after every controversial vote some people saw fit to call in and berate whoever picked up the phone. A group unhappy with our policy on Central America distributed posters that branded us accomplices to murder. One quickly recognizes that arguing with such entrenched opponents only makes matters worse: it wastes your time and gives them more ammunition to use against you. To handle such persons, remember that you'll never change their minds—these are the people who have made up their minds already and wouldn't want to be confused by the facts—and that you're never going to please everyone, nor should you bother trying. Keep your composure, terminate the conversation as

124

quickly as possible and save your energy for more productive activities.

Constituents with personal concerns are often no kinder. The impatient person whose information request was mishandled doesn't care about the backlog of assignments mounting on your desk because an intern has been out sick, or that you haven't been home for dinner all week, or that you're responsible for preparing the briefing for the congressman's event that evening. And you can't give impolite constituents the tongue-lashing they may deserve, lest you turn them against your boss. That's where the thick skin comes in again, as you resist the urge to shout back and instead discipline yourself not to descend to the same unmannerly behavior as the caller.

I became known in our office as the expert in terminating those seemingly interminable calls, usually by injecting a quick "Thank you for sharing your thoughts, rest assured they will be passed on to the congressman and you will receive a reply, have a good day" and then hanging up. About once a year I brazenly hung up on a constituent in the middle of his or her tirade, but only after I had concluded that the caller was not of sound mind or was engaging in repetitive monologue without permitting interruption. Such constituents provide the acid test of one's compassion. I always said that anyone who didn't have the heart to pity and pray for such persons should get out of public-sector work; but that didn't mean I would pointlessly expend time on them that could fruitfully be used giving real assistance to someone else.

One memorable caller insisted that the Federal Communications Commission was transmitting unwanted signals to her through her radio. I patiently listened and indicated that without documentation we could do little to help but that if she gave us specifics in writing we would do what we could. Usually the interaction ends there, but this woman followed up with a letter—lacking specifics, of course. Attempting to be sensitive to the world of a schizophrenic, I drafted a diplomatic reply indicating that, although I had no doubt that the experience was very real for her, we could not assist her without independently verifiable evidence.

A year later this woman started calling again, then showed up at the office unannounced. When I offered her an appointment, she walked out on me and rewarded my patience by calling everyone she could think of to report how miserably our office had treated her. Happily my superiors believed my side of the story, as they did on another occasion when a constituent unhappy with my answers to her demands claimed I had requested sexual favors in exchange for my assistance. But I had trouble accepting that my sincere efforts to help would sometimes be recompensed by such ill will.

Anyone who has done customer service for a living can probably relate to my experiences (and anyone who has labored faithfully at a psychiatric hospital will find my laments quite inconsequential by comparison). Constituent service is basically a specialized form of customer service, intensified by the fact that dissatisfied constituents, more than disgruntled store patrons who might call the manager or just not return to the store, have a socially acceptable means (the next campaign) to work actively for the termination of your job.

As constituent service resembles customer service, so grassroots campaign work resembles telemarketing—and no field requires a thicker skin than that one. Political "cold calling" isn't quite as bad as telemarketing, in that you're asking people only for their vote, not their money. (Campaign fundraising calls to lists of known supporters are usually contracted out to professional telemarketing firms, because of the difficulty in finding volunteers willing to handle the assignment.) But you will need to be emotionally prepared for that small minority of citizens who refuse to act civilly toward their neighbor and who instead slam the door in your face or hang up on you, sometimes with cruel comments like "I always vote against candidates who disturb my privacy."

Broad Shoulders

Next, you will want strong shoulders both to accept the weight of responsibility laid upon you and to take firm, decisive, even aggressive steps on behalf of the positions and candidates you support.

Like the offensive linemen on a football team, you must be prepared to do the hard work in the trenches and let someone else take the glory. Unless you become the candidate, the team of which you are a part does not bear your name, nor will your name appear on the ballot on election day. If your ego can't tolerate someone else taking credit for your good work, you don't belong in this field. In fact, a good politician intentionally deflects all credit toward that someone else. I constantly reminded persons who appreciated my service that they should thank not me but the congressman who set the office policies that directed me to do what I was doing.

On the other hand, if something goes wrong you must be prepared to accept the blame or even dismissal for the team's benefit. If the candidate's political survival entails repudiating the activity in which you have engaged, you may be expected to offer your resignation and to refrain from defending your own reputation by protesting that the boss approved of the policy. Had Rick Santorum felt the need to fire me over the *New Yorker* escapade, I would have been expected to depart without a whimper. If you can't stand the risk of being fired should you ever happen to be the fittest nominee for the role of scapegoat, don't take on much responsibility.

Don't think that candidates and officeholders have it easier,

127

though. They often must swallow hard and remember Harry Truman's motto, "The buck stops here." They may indeed have had no knowledge of a staffer's misdeed until long after it happened, but sometimes to admit they didn't know what was going on would be more embarrassing than to defend it.

I remember preparing the press release that displayed Rick Santorum's commitment to budget-cutting by listing the programs he would eliminate. "Are you sure Rick wants to eliminate the Small Business Administration?" I inquired, rather surprised, of the campaign staffer who gave me the list. It turned out that Santorum had received the list from a Washington think tank and had passed it on to the campaign staffer for review, not intending to endorse all the specific proposals. But the message became garbled, and before I got the story straight I had already sent the release out to local media, announcing that candidate Santorum wanted to cut the SBA. Happily that was one of the releases nobody noticed. Otherwise we would have had quite a time trying to present a "sorry, campaign staff goofed" alibi that sounds all too convenient after the negative feedback has already begun.

Broad shoulders will also keep you from being a pushover, susceptible to persuasion because you don't want to hurt anyone's feelings. You don't want to agree to take a yard sign from the first candidate who knocks on your door, before you know what he stands for or who else is running, just because he asked and you hate to say no. If you back one side of an issue at a friend's request, what will you say to your other friend when you learn she's advocating for the other side?

It's too easy to agree with whoever is talking to you at the moment, without considering the consequences. Better to buy time by declining to make an immediate commitment until you are sure you believe the position you have been asked to support. The respect you gain by acting deliberately and demonstrating that you stick to your commitments far outweighs the occasional scorn you may receive from short-sighted, fair-weather friends who can't sway you to their position. It is permissible to change your mind—but not too often. When you do, the change should clearly represent a thoughtful reconsideration of your views, not a repudiation of your own hasty, foolish actions.

Politics involves disagreement and confrontation. The person willing to compromise anything stands for nothing. You must be ready to stand firmly for what you believe—and, while never belittling your opponents, you must not be hesitant to demolish their positions mercilessly. Like a skillful boxer or a wild animal, you must discern when to lie in wait and when to pounce. In any public interaction (by which I mean anything from a formal debate to an office party where a coworker criticizes your candidate), remember that your goal is not to change your opponent's mind—which almost never happens—but to win over the uncommitted audience. The point where your adversary offers an easily dismantled argument is the time not to feel pity but to pounce with your rebuttal.

I once had the unenviable task of representing my congressman at a meeting in a comfortable suburban community under consideration as a site for new, low-income public housing. Several hundred citizens packed the hall to declare vociferously that they wanted no public housing in their community. Although we opposed the construction of new public housing, this project had resulted from a protracted lawsuit and we could do little to stop it. I tried valiantly to offer the residents constructive suggestions, but any ideas on how they might be able to coexist with the development brought raucous boos down upon me. One alternative proposal did emerge from the audience, and I needed my broad shoulders to resist committing my boss's endorsement on the spot (we did, in fact, decide later to support it).

Toward the close of the meeting one irate resident got dirty and asked me where I lived and whether my town had any public housing. It was an awkward moment, because, although my house is smaller than most of the homes in the community where we were meeting, it sits in the corner of a relatively affluent suburb with no public housing. However, I perceived that I could win by taking the offensive. After acknowledging where I lived, I pointed out the extent of my own involvement in distressed communities and blasted the questioner for lodging an inappropriate, irrelevant personal attack that did nothing to solve the problem. The unexpected applause confirmed my judgment that by putting one questioner to shame I could solidify the rest of the audience's respect for our position.

Big Head

The politician with broad shoulders stands straight and tall, self-assured, full of confidence and ambition, with a secure but not an oversized ego. A large ego is not the kind of "big head" I have in mind as the next aspect of the politician's physique; on the contrary, the appearance of self-centeredness can be disastrous. Nor do I mean a high IQ, though that can certainly be helpful. Rather, you'll want a head large enough to store all the names, faces and facts you'll have to recall.

The most effective means of political persuasion is personal attention. Thus you can make yourself a local party standout by getting to know your neighbors—not only who they are, but how they think and what's important to them. Ideally, a local party worker should know every voter in his or her own precinct, or at least those of the same party, and what it takes to motivate each person to support a candidate. (For example: "Jane owns a small business so I'll tell her about the candidate with a business background"; "John always complains about taxes so I'll recruit him to work for the candidates who have pledged not to raise taxes.")

Of course, in a precinct of several hundred households you'll

130

never achieve the ideal, but the more people you know, the better. If you acquire this kind of familiarity with even half your neighbors, you'll be on your way to stardom the first time you take a candidate door to door through your subdivision and he or she marvels at your ability to tailor the right part of the candidate's message to each person you know. You also want to recognize as many people as possible if you serve as a poll worker on election day, and you want to know (as can be determined from voting records) who votes regularly and who needs a reminder call to get them to the polls. If you don't have an encyclopedic memory, keep a card file or database with your neighbors' names, addresses and other pertinent information and review it to refresh your memory before you cover the polls or canvass the neighborhood.

I work very hard at remembering names to compensate for my most embarrassing shortcoming: I cannot recognize faces. I didn't recognize my wife after she got new eyeglasses. "Give me a few months and I'll forget any face," I've had to apologize countless times to acquaintances surprised by my blank stare when I encountered them in public. I know how essential it is for a good politician to "work the room" at public events, personally greeting everyone he or she knows, but unfortunately I can't do it unless people are wearing name tags. In advance of such events I anticipate whom I expect to see there, both to increase my chance of recognizing them and so that I can prepare something intelligent to say if I meet them. The sweetest music in any citizen's ear, besides the sound of his or her own name, is a comment that suggests you know about and appreciate what he or she is doing.

I don't have an encyclopedic memory either, but my capacity (assisted by frequent reference to my Rolodex and address book) to keep a lot of people in my head has been politically beneficial in many ways. On the government side, I have won many friends by keeping them in my mental file and remembering to send

131

them grant solicitations or other information that would interest them. Recipients often seemed amazingly grateful just that someone in their congressman's office thought of them frequently enough to send them this material. Also, we solved many constituent problems because I remembered or had a file on someone who could help find an answer to that particular question. On the campaign side, I was regularly called upon to recommend volunteers for various activities, and as I gained a reputation for having a large bank of contacts, other candidates began seeking my help. As we have noted earlier, the more one's services are in demand, the more influence one can exert.

If you want to make politics a career, you'll also need a big head to manage all the issues you or your boss must address. It's hard to represent a legislator or a candidate, let alone be one, if when asked about a current issue you can't remember the facts you learned at the last briefing. You'll never be able to retain every useful item—I've had my share of "I forgot, did the House already pass its crime bill or was that the Senate?"—but you need to discipline yourself to remember key points on the main issues. I believe the best measurement of when you've learned enough, as we noted when describing campaign coffees in chapter four, is whether you can admit "I don't know" when you don't know something, without fearing that your ignorance will be a source of political embarrassment.

Big Ears

After the sound of their own name or praise of their achievements, the next sweetest music to most people's ears is the sound of their own voice. People love to talk, and even more so if they think someone is listening. They usually don't care so much whether you agree with them, as long as you listen to them and respond to their deepest concerns.

We all know politicians must be good talkers, but we often

neglect the importance of good listening. Those who interrupt, talk too long or talk too much communicate an image of self-centeredness that does not inspire loyalty. Those who listen well project an image of humility and concern for others, two essential components of mature leadership.

Working in a congressional office, one becomes amazed at the number of people who seem to have nothing better to do than call regularly to comment on the issue of the day, or who phone the office with a specific problem yet somehow digress into relating their life story. The hostile callers aren't the biggest problem—you can cut them off quickly without causing any harm. It's the friendly ones, whom you don't want to offend, who pose the greatest challenge. Two such calls, plus the sanity break required to recover from each of them, can rob an hour or more from every workday.

I actually began keeping reading material within reach so that, on those occasions when I could find no way to cut off a long-winded caller, I could catch up on my reading while waiting for the constituent to stop talking. But even then I tried to listen closely enough (or I tuned back in at the end of the monologue and asked a few questions) in order to identify how I could best respond.

Your willingness to offer help is the best proof that you are listening and that you care, so it is always wise to complete the conversation by agreeing upon some specific action you will take. A frustrated mother who calls to complain about the treatment her child is receiving at the county jail will not take kindly to a curt "sorry, that's not our jurisdiction" cutoff. But after twenty minutes of pouring out her griefs, if you offer to make sure that anything she sends is forwarded to the jail warden's personal attention, she may appreciate your sincere concern and accept graciously your explanation that you don't have the power to do anything more than that.

When dealing with a voter face to face rather than on the phone, you don't have the option of getting other work done while half-listening. Instead you have to indulge the speaker up to the point where any reasonable observer would acknowledge you have been more than patient. If you are a legislator, that amount of time might be five or ten minutes. At one of Congressman Santorum's town meetings the first person who asked to comment was an elderly man who spoke slowly and repetitively, but without pausing, for seven minutes on a local zoning dispute. When Santorum finally broke in with "Sir, do you have a question?" no one could fault him for failing to listen, though some must have wished he could have interrupted six minutes earlier!

If you are a staff member or campaign volunteer with fewer responsibilities and no aide to drag you out, saying, "Congressman, I know you want to talk, but we have to get to another meeting," you may need to give an hour or two of your life to a talkative complainer, no matter how incoherent the complaint may be. If you chafe at the thought of expending your time in so inefficient a fashion, remember that you are helping the cause by guaranteeing that, if the constituent next resorts to contacting the media and claiming you refused to help, your office will have no difficulty demonstrating that the constituent is nuts.

Smooth Lips

Politicians are regularly accused of telling people what they want to hear. I admit, I am guilty as charged. No, I don't consciously make contradictory statements in different settings; that tactic is not only dishonest but usually backfires in a short time as your conflicting comments collide along the grapevine. The smooth lips of a good politician don't have to tell lies. Rather, they win friends by having something nice to say to everyone.

Political figures have an enormous number of brief conversations with the public—at party meetings, receptions, grand openings, community days. If you have smooth lips, you can build good will with each acquaintance you encounter in these contexts through a well-placed compliment or a comment that acknowledges the importance of what that person is doing. Such words both help the recipient feel appreciated and build a valuable presumption that you and the person complimented have shared interests. That presumption in turn develops an increased desire to put or keep you (or your boss) in office.

Whenever I visited with community leaders, I went informed of their activities and armed with sweet words. I praised newly elected officials for their diligent campaigning while thanking outgoing council members for their leadership on local projects. When presenting a flag to a community full of contentious debate on municipal issues, I lauded the town board and the citizens for their energetic participation in the democratic process that has made America great. (Politics is more fun when you don't have to take sides.) I always tried to provide enough specificity so that my words would be received as genuine and heartfelt, not as empty platitudes. And I always searched for compliments I could offer in full sincerity, since it's much easier to sound sincere when you *are* sincere.

I also strove to connect with every individual or group audience by relating some part of my background that helped me appreciate or value their activity. Having an eclectic background helped considerably in that regard. To African-American groups I cited my years of inner-city youth soccer coaching; among disabilities advocates I noted the impact my summer as counselor at a camp for persons with disabilities had on my life; around teachers my autobiographical highlight was that I had intended to enter teaching before a political career fell in my lap; and so on.

To complete your positive verbal presentation, your smooth lips must also produce smooth speech. Whether in public or in

135

private, stammering speech full of stumbles and "you know's" marks you as unprepared, unprofessional and unsure of yourself. If you don't have public speaking experience, get some. Practice speaking to friends or to the mirror until you can deliver a short speech comfortably without depending on a written text. If you don't like public speaking, then stay behind the scenes; this weakness alone can sabotage an otherwise solid politician.

Strong Heart

Campaigns are not for the faint-hearted. The hectic pace calls for good health and plenty of adrenaline to put off sleeping until after election night. During the final weeks you must endure the stress of devoting every available hour to campaign work, doing everything as fast as possible, and trying not to faint when you see how many mistakes you or your fellow coworkers are making in your haste and inexperience. There are always more tasks to complete and more people to contact—and, notwithstanding the sophistication of modern polling, you never know for sure if you have done enough until election night, at which time it is too late to atone for prior omissions.

I vividly remember the fear I felt ten days before the end of my first campaign experience. It appeared at that point that we were in a close race, and I was irrationally terrified that one poorly chosen comment or dropped assignment by the press secretary (me) might spoil two years of work by the candidate and hundreds of supporters. Happily, we had no media embarrassments and I reached election day in good conscience, knowing that I had done all I could do, as well as I knew how. Reflecting on the agony you would feel if you gave less than your best and your candidate lost narrowly should keep you from slacking off until the last vote is cast. But no heart attacks in early November, please.

A strong heart also represents the loyalty required of a good politician. As a team player you may have to defend votes or positions with which you personally disagree. Refuting the arguments of your informed adversaries and tolerating ridicule from less polite opponents is hard anytime, but even more so when you'd like to say, "I agree with you." Furthermore, if you want to progress very far, you will have to accept the control politics comes to exert over your personal life, because everything you do—where you worship, your community activities, your sources of amusement—can reflect upon your boss. You will be compelled to cultivate certain friendships (with influential persons and political supporters) and avoid others (with protesters and extremists). You must contemplate the political implications of everything you do. Your life is a fishbowl. If you don't like it, don't seek a job or a leadership position in politics.

Finally, you will need a strong heart to withstand the injustice, fickleness and plain luck that play a larger role in politics than you may think. You may campaign tirelessly for a year, only to see your efforts undermined by an independent protest candidate who enters the race at the last minute and steals just enough votes from you to help the incumbent stay in office. You may spend thousands of dollars only to lose because of the random drawing that determined your low ballot position (the first position on the ballot in a crowded field is estimated to be worth one or two percentage points, as uninformed voters select the first name they recognize). Your opponent may defeat you with underhanded tactics or outright lies that go undiscovered until after the votes have been counted. The victims of the criminal activities now known as Watergate may have felt vindicated by the events of 1974, but in 1972 they were hopelessly obliterated in a presidential election.

Sometimes good prevails; at other times it prevails belatedly; at still other times it can only bemoan injustice. You must be ready to shake off those disappointments and continue caring compassionately about people and about righteousness, knowing that to slink back into disillusionment and apathy will serve only to help evil win more often.

If You Want to Run

Have you caught the bug yet? Most political workers entertain at some point the tempting thought of actually running for office themselves. I used to joke, without much exaggeration, that when I asked applicants for congressional internships about their aspirations, half said they wanted to be a member of Congress and the other half wanted to end up in the U.S. Senate.

I know of no vocation that demands a wider range of skills than running for elective office. There is no shame in discovering that you are better equipped to serve as an aide than as a candidate. Assisting a representative, though far less visible a role, is just as honorable a calling as being (or trying to become) the representative. Many personality types—dry academics, reluctant speakers and quiet servants who shun the limelight, to name a few—are best advised to acknowledge from the start that they will not make good candidates.

Nevertheless, whether you are contemplating a run yourself or just evaluating other hopefuls who seek your support, you'll want to know what makes a good candidate. Beyond all the traits already discussed in this chapter, look for these fifteen:

Analytical ability. Can the candidate analyze issues quickly and thoroughly and present a position coherently?

Values. Does the candidate share your core values and your positions on the issues of greatest importance to you?

Diplomacy. Does the candidate behave in such a way as to make lots of friends and few enemies?

Salesmanship. Can the candidate unapologetically look people in the eye and ask for their support or their money?

Civic knowledge. Does the candidate illustrate familiarity with the communities and neighborhoods where the election will be contested, along with their local leaders?

Contacts. Does the candidate already know many persons who will make a substantial contribution to the campaign and who can influence other contributors? One friend considers this qualification so crucial that his first question to any potential candidate is "Who's on your finance committee?"

Delegating. The candidate personally cannot do everything in a campaign. Can he or she wisely delegate tasks, in the right amounts and to the right people?

Leadership qualities. Does the candidate inspire persons to follow, trust and recommend him or her as a leader?

Character. Is the candidate without serious moral flaws?

Organization. Can the candidate organize, prioritize and carry out the complex array of tasks a campaign entails?

Realism. Does the candidate take tempered stances and avoid pronouncements so unpopular as to make electoral success impossible?

Appearance. Are the candidate's physical appearance, dress and voice quality attractive, or at least pleasant enough to make a positive impression?

Drive. My wife has provided an unforgettable description, derived from close observation, of running for Congress: "It's one year of no income and no family time, at the end of which either you lose or you win the reward of two more years of no family time." The demands are less intensive at the state or local level, but they remain substantial. Has the candidate reasonably assessed the financial and personal costs of running, and does he or she have the drive to stick with it day after day, resisting fatigue and discouragement?

Campaign plan. Does the candidate show a clear sense of what must be done in order to win and how he or she intends to do it?

Humility. This long list should prove that anyone who claims to be an ideal candidate possesses too large an ego to be fit for public office.

9

CAN RELIGION & POLITICS MIX?

. . . .

*T*he Far Right Marches into School Governance," warned the cover of *The School Administrator,* a magazine for public-school educators, in 1993. On the inside of this publication, articles exposed efforts by conservative Christians to control their schools' policies by gaining a majority on their local school board. The Christians' agenda, according to the articles, was to impose creationism upon science classes, restore school prayer, eliminate offensive literature and hamstring sex education. Although the magazine printed statements by two leaders of Christian organizations who argued that they had a much broader and more mainstream vision, the other articles depicted a tightly knit network of narrow-minded, sectarian extremists cleverly coached to conceal their oddities until after they got elected

Since the late 1970s, when conservative Christians emerged as a sufficiently powerful force in American politics to gain a label as the Christian Right, such unflattering assessments have proliferated. Detractors have attacked not only the Christian Right's ideology but also its style, calling it uncivil, divisive, self-righteous and condemnatory, along with a few less charitable epithets.

Although it may seem difficult to brand these Christians' lack of tolerance intolerable without sounding a bit intolerant oneself, that difficulty has not stopped critics from trying. Here's a typical example, taken from a speech by philanthropist Teresa Heinz, formerly the wife of the late Pennsylvania senator John Heinz and now married to Massachusetts senator John Kerry: "Rather than preach Christ's gospel of love and tolerance, this group broadcasts its hatred for homosexuals and liberals and minorities and feminists. The movement calls itself Christian, but its appeal is to dark corners of the human soul—fear, loathing, the desire for uniformity, the need for conformity."

To call the debate over the role of religious believers in politics a hot one would, as one can judge from the tone of the criticisms just quoted, be an understatement. But it is one from which we neither can nor should walk away. We *can't* ignore the issue, because too many Americans are insisting on connecting their faith with their politics and ignoring their opponents' protests that "separation of church and state" makes it illegitimate for them to do so. The issue will remain with us whether we like it or not, and if we don't handle it wisely it may tear our society apart in hostile "culture wars" among firmly entrenched, unyielding factions whose values cannot be reconciled with each other. As the violence at abortion clinics has reminded us, these culture wars strike too close to the most cherished beliefs of too many people to remain just verbal wars indefinitely if not defused.

But neither should we *want* to ignore this issue, for a wise linkage of religion and politics is eminently desirable. The widespread acknowledgment—in the debates over welfare reform, for example—that public policy cannot be value-free has spurred a broad-based effort to recover the contribution religious values can and must make to the public good, even in a pluralistic society. The popularity of Stephen Carter's *The Culture of Disbelief,* which argued this point and was favorably cited by President and Mrs. Clinton after its release in 1994, shows that the concern to reinject religious-based values into public life extends far beyond the Christian Right. (Carter himself is an African-American with liberal political leanings.)

This concluding chapter is at points somewhat more complex than the preceding ones, since describing how properly to relate religion and politics entails deeper philosophical considerations than those needed to explain how to run for office. But you will have to be prepared to address this issue if you intend to do sensitive, honest politics in America today. Whatever your own stance regarding spiritual faith and its political implications, you will want to know

☐ that not all religious believers hold the same political views
☐ how to balance the perspectives of religious and nonreligious persons in matters of public policy
☐ how persons of faith should and should not communicate their views in public debate
☐ how religious and nonreligious persons can interact respectfully and constructively in the civil sphere

Although the principles discussed in this chapter are broadly applicable, I will examine them with primary relation to the Christian Right, since this religious group has aroused the lion's share of the controversy.

Why the Bad Rap?

Does the Christian Right, often charged with connecting religion and politics in a narrowly sectarian, socially harmful way, deserve the bad rap it has received? Not always, but sometimes.

To some extent, the bad rap on politically active conservative Christians is simply a testimony to their success. They have gained enough influence and helped win enough campaigns that their ideological opponents have had to mount a rhetorical counterattack. In democratic elections, candidates try to position themselves at the center and their opponents at the radical fringe of popular opinion. Thus it should be no surprise that political moderates and liberals have attempted to pin the label "far right" on virtually anyone who votes prolife and welcomes the Christian Coalition's support. Christian conservatives, after all, have been just as anxious to portray their opposition as "far left."

The critics wouldn't stick with this tactic for long, however, if it never worked. The tactic works because conservative Christians have behaved frequently enough in ways that make the tags of extremism and intolerance credible to the general public. Their boasts of political muscle and more than sporadic references to what will happen when Christians "take over" reflect a propensity to build broader alliances only reluctantly while preferring to secure power as a bloc. This behavior, though somewhat more restrained in recent years, has fostered mutual distrust, especially within Republican circles where party regulars have feared Christian Right attempts to take over the party structure. It has also encouraged those who do not consider themselves that kind of Christian to view these conservatives as a threat.

These leaders should have been able to do better, since their single most visible stance—their prolife advocacy—is a costly, selfless activity on behalf of the helpless (i.e., unborn children who cannot protect themselves) and which brings personal gain to virtually none of the advocates. But they have appealed too often to their own religious motivations and too seldom to the public good. As a result, a large portion of America finds harsh critics like Teresa Heinz accurate, forcing candidates to walk a tightrope as they bid for conservative Christian support, yet distance themselves from the Christian Right in public discourse. The campaign for the 1996 Republican presidential nomination has left us ample evidence of such tightrope-walking.

The charge trumpeted by those *School Administrator* magazine articles—that conservative Christians run as stealth candidates who hide their real intentions until after they have snuck into office—is also credible. Not only have some professing Christians behaved in this way, but they openly teach others to do so. One conservative political consultant has written, in a book intended to teach grassroots politics to Christians, that since the media often portray Christian candidates in an unfavorable light, "it may be wiser not to totally reveal yourself until after elected." Christians are campaigning to get elected and then governing in a manner so different from their campaign as to cause voters to feel they have been deceived. This is hardly the way either to honor the Christian gospel or to extend one's career of public service beyond a single controversial term.

I must confess to feeling defensive about these tactics, because as an evangelical Christian who holds generally conservative political views I am associated with such behavior whether I myself engage in it or not. Beyond any insecurities about my own image, however, I would desire that the involvement of Christians in politics might turn people toward, not away from, the gospel. Let's look at what Christians, especially those controversial conservative ones, have been doing and how they can make their politics both more truly Christian and more successful. We will then approach the issue of religion and politics from the nonreligious person's perspective.

Not All Christians Are Right

The hubbub surrounding the Christian Right has left many people with the false impression that all politically active Christians

145

are ideologically conservative. Actually, for most of this century, conservative Christians were seldom seen in U.S. politics at all. The primary religious voice in the political realm was that of the mainline Protestant church leaders who still hoped for worldly progress through social action and who translated their faith into support for such causes as racial equality. Evangelicals and fundamentalists, abandoning the tradition of social activism that had typified their progressive nineteenth-century predecessors, had largely withdrawn from politics. They were too pessimistic about achieving meaningful social change in that way; instead they concentrated on saving souls through their spiritual gospel and waited for the second coming of Christ (which many of them expected would come soon).

All of that changed in the 1970s, but not because religious conservatives had become optimistic about politics. The Christian Right arose because its members felt their government was becoming increasingly hostile to their values. Though a few of its leaders imagined that national political renewal could restore America to God, most wanted to protect their personal freedoms (especially religious freedom) and to fight the erosion of America's morality (especially sexual morality). For them politics remained an unfortunate, albeit now necessary, diversion from their main task of soul-saving. As a result they acted in a heavily reactionary way, committed to fighting off bad ideas rather than devoting themselves to constructing and living out a positive vision of public service through politics.

This emotional call to resist the encroachments of an ever more secularized government caused the Christian Right to grow rapidly into the most powerful religious-based force in American politics. But even though this movement has seized most of the attention, committed Christians can still be found at all places on the political spectrum today, not just on the right. Christian political theorist James Skillen, in his book *The Scattered Voice: Chris-*

146

tians at Odds in the Public Square, identifies seven distinct, prominent schools of thought, ranging from libertarian to liberal. Those who lean toward the left, though less frequently identified as "religious" leaders (even if they are ordained ministers), are just as intentionally Christian in their thinking.

The political differences among Christians can be illuminated, much as we explained the divide between the parties in chapter six, by asking how one views government's role. Western religion has historically emphasized both individual responsibility before God and social responsibility to create a just human order that treats all persons fairly. These duties can be complementary; after all, working for social justice becomes part of every believer's individual responsibility. But they also can collide, in the sense that using the powers of government to achieve social *justice* can require limits on individuals' *freedom* to live as they see fit. To create opportunities for minorities, for instance, we may have to exclude whites from certain positions. To fund summer jobs for needy youths we must take money, by taxation, from persons who might have used that money to educate their own children better.

The freedom-versus-justice terminology would of course need some refinement to avoid oversimplification; religious liberals sometimes cast themselves as protectors of freedoms (those of convicted criminals or Central American refugees, for example) that conservatives would curtail. But, in general, religious liberals stress government's role in ensuring social justice, while conservatives want government to protect individual freedom. Conservatives believe more strongly in letting *individuals*—not government—take care of themselves, their families and (where necessary) their neighbors.

I would hate to think that American evangelicals base their policies on self-interest, but I do find that they tend to generalize from their experience, which is predominantly an experience of

147

stable, middle-class families who can fend for themselves, perhaps with a little help from the church benevolence fund should a crisis arise. As a result, they have held government solutions in disfavor, and their distrust only increases when they perceive government as trying to control their lives.

In this way conservative religion, when awakened to political involvement, can become largely a bastion of conservative politics. It sees the individual, not government, as the source of meaningful social change. Although conservative Christians are not politically monolithic, the religious left is dwarfed by the ability of groups like the Christian Coalition to take their voter guides into thousands of conservative churches with full confidence that this information will sway the great majority of members of those congregations toward, not away from, the group's favored candidates. The left can respond in kind only by calling upon liberal Christians and Jews, whose level of engagement seldom approaches that of conservative evangelicals or prolife Catholics, and upon the black church, where racial and economic issues have made social justice through government intervention a far more favorable concept than it is among white evangelicals.

Over time the Christian Right—partly through honest reflection and partly out of a pragmatic desire to shake off that "extremist" tag—has become more caring and more sophisticated. The movement is, on the whole, more willing now to acknowledge that others can truly hold the same faith without arriving at the same political conclusions. But it still struggles to determine how best to participate politically as Christians in a society where many citizens do not hold the same theological foundation. Whereas moderate and liberal Christians tend to obliterate any signs of Christian distinctiveness from their advocacy, conservative Christians often tend toward trying to use the civil government to impose Christianity on non-Christian citizens.

148

I believe there is a more fully Christian way to approach political involvement, one that can bridge the gap between religious and nonreligious persons without forcing either group to compromise its principles—and, from the Christian perspective, one that offers greater potential for success both politically and spiritually.

How Believers Should Integrate Religion and Politics

In his New Testament letter to young Timothy, the apostle Paul writes:

> I urge that supplications, prayers, intercessions, and thanksgivings be made for everyone, for kings and all who are in high positions, so that we may lead a quiet and peaceable life in all godliness and dignity. This is right and is acceptable in the sight of God our Savior, who desires everyone to be saved and to come to the knowledge of the truth. (1 Timothy 2:1-4)

The writers of the New Testament were very concerned about how their government operated, but not because they wanted to make it a vehicle for converting people. They knew that government was God-ordained (whether directed by people of faith or not), and they prayed for a government that would permit the church to preach the gospel. In doing so they showed a clear grasp of the distinction between the two institutions.

For Christians, the *church* is entrusted with the message of spiritual salvation and is responsible for seeking to bring others to accept this message. The church pursues this task by persuasion, not coercion, since a genuine inward spiritual commitment cannot be created by outward compulsion. Membership is restricted to believers, but it is strictly voluntary, and the church has no grounds for punitive action against persons who choose not to join.

In contrast, *civil government* (the state) must rule over and serve all persons, whatever their religious faith. It carries the power of

149

coercion, without which it could not maintain order, but it should regulate only actions, not beliefs. Its job is to foster the outward behaviors necessary to maintain a civil society, but not to stipulate inward allegiance. We use a Pledge of Allegiance to promote civil harmony, but we do not punish those who refuse to repeat it.

People can justifiably be required to behave in ways essential to maintaining civil order, but they should be only persuaded, not compelled by force of law, toward religious adherence. Therefore—contrary to the widespread expectation that Christians in politics will impose their religious views on others—a genuinely Christian worldview will not advocate any civil law that non-Christians could not also perceive as just.

Government can be *compatible* with Christianity without being explicitly Christian, and it is this compatibility for which Christians should strive. They should desire a government that permits them to preach the gospel, but not one that specifically favors Christians over non-Christians in any way (such as by allowing only Christians to hold office, or by granting tax exemption to churches but not to Hindu temples, or by encouraging sectarian public prayers).

This does not mean that Christians should stop looking to the Bible for guidance on how to build a good society; many of our nation's founders, even the deist Thomas Jefferson, looked there. It does mean that if a Christian cannot defend a proposal without using the Bible, he or she has no grounds for compelling someone who doesn't believe the Bible to obey it as civil law.

Some fear that this approach forces Christians to compromise their views. On the contrary, it enables them to act with clarity and consistency. Christians who would never dream of requiring religious observance by nonbelievers at their workplace or in their community-service organizations have inconsistently held to a sectarian conception of civil government, claiming that it should favor Christianity. When they do so, however sincere their zeal for moral righteousness, they misunderstand the purpose of government, misuse its power and alienate unbelievers rather than winning them over through respectful service.

Those who want government to favor Christians actually violate the golden rule. They would recognize this if they lived in a country, such as many Muslim nations, China or even Japan, where Christianity suffers unequal treatment as a minority religion. A culturally dominant faith that wields civil power in this way is not likely to earn respect or allegiance from persons of other faiths. In direct contrast, one of the best ways for Christians to present a positive witness in public life is to seek to uphold the civil rights of all persons, whatever their faith.

Keeping sectarian preferences out of public debate does not mean the total exclusion of God. Persons of faith may justifiably appeal, in nonsectarian fashion, to the existence of a Creator as the foundation of our shared morality and the source of our rights and responsibilities. This type of appeal is different because it depends not on any special revelation such as the Bible, but on the virtually universal acknowledgment that the awareness of a Creator to whom we owe our being should be apparent to anyone who looks at the world honestly. (The apostle Paul made this point in Romans 1:18-20 and 2:12-16, but if this argument is internally consistent its truth should be perceived with or without the explicitly Christian evidence!)

Even the tiny minority that refuses to acknowledge a Creator should be placated by the assurance that we won't compel them to pray as long as they don't keep the rest of us from referring to what we consider the basis for our moral responsibility. The consensus on this point is essentially uncontested, however, as evidenced by the fact that no one is fighting to amend the Declaration of Independence, our nation's most prominent example of Creator-talk. Even while rejecting the sectarian strife that had

151

torn Europe, the Declaration's authors did not hesitate to appeal to deity in nonsectarian terms three times, as Creator, Supreme Judge and Divine Providence. Without invoking any specifically Christian language, they based the Declaration's "self-evident truths" and "inalienable rights" on all persons' responsibility to a Creator who has endowed us with those rights.

This appeal to a Creator, which is consistent with conscience but not dependent on any particular religious revelation, provides the needed transcendent moral foundation for civil law while also avoiding the twin pitfalls of secularism and sectarianism, neither of which can sustain a sense of moral responsibility in a pluralistic nation. Without this nonsectarian acknowledgment of God, our nation's moral foundation makes little sense. Can one imagine the Founding Fathers stating that we were endowed with inalienable rights by a Big Bang?

A Philosophy of Servanthood

In the Gospel of Matthew we read the words of Jesus:

> You know that the rulers of the Gentiles lord it over them, and their great ones are tyrants over them. It will not be so among you; but whoever wishes to be great among you must be your servant, and whoever wishes to be first among you must be your slave. (Matthew 20:25-27)

Had the Christian Right clearly articulated from its inception a thorough philosophy of public engagement like the one I have outlined in the previous section, it might not have provoked such a backlash from opponents—many of whom are also committed Christians—who saw a modern Inquisition in the making. In fairness, however, let us recall that the early Christian Right leaders became active in politics reluctantly, rather suddenly, without a lifetime of philosophical reflection on the topic, and with a deep conviction that the secular world was putting them on the defensive. That conviction was, if exaggerated, essentially accurate, and their entry into the fray over abortion and sexuality could not help but arouse controversy. Nevertheless, had they spoken from a consistent philosophical foundation that showed clearly they had no intention to Christianize civil government, they might not have gained such high negative ratings.

Along with this philosophy of nonsectarian public involvement, Christians have too often lacked sufficiently servantlike motivation. They have seen politics as a means to wrest power from the godless rather than to serve one's neighbor, and as a result they have engaged too much in divisive verbiage and have listened too little to the real needs of others.

Ironically, not only should "politics as servanthood" be a cornerstone of Christian action—in fact, Christians should be the best public servants, because they should be the people least bound to their own self-interest—but those who adopt this style tend to gain the public's trust and thus accrue more power along the way besides. My own experience, though I have lived out my principles only imperfectly, has reinforced this conviction.

When I joined the Republican party I resolved to earn whatever opportunities came my way by working hard for a candidate whom I could support. As a press secretary for a congressional campaign, I did my job faithfully and chose my words carefully, so that by election day I was known in local Republican circles for my loyalty and my reliable performance.

After I joined my newly elected congressman's district office staff, for the next four years the district's needs set my agenda. I spoke with people not about the issues of greatest import to me, but about what was important to them. My deep Christian concern to serve others, combined with my wife's tolerance of my long work hours, enabled me to respond to constituent needs more thoroughly and sensitively than most staff. By caring about people's problems in this way I gained more opportunities to share my faith meaningfully than if I had devoted my energies

153

to advancing a narrowly Christian policy agenda. My deeds spoke more loudly than my words.

As for my Christian responsibility to share my faith, I did it judiciously on official time, when explaining my motivation to go beyond the call of duty in public service, and more explicitly on private time. Dozens of constituents, if they didn't find out any other way, learned of my spiritual motivations each year from my Christmas letter.

Means Rather Than Ends
In Romans 15:7 Paul writes,

Welcome one another, therefore, just as Christ has welcomed you, for the glory of God.

By placing their political zeal within a broader context of humble public service, Christians also gain a healthy dose of humility about their own political views. Mature Christians still articulate their own stances with passion, but they are also good listeners who give intense and careful consideration to opposing views. They sincerely want to understand why others think differently, and, knowing their own imperfections, they do not insist dogmatically that their own position is perfectly right. Instead they open themselves honestly to the reality that they do not always hear God's voice clearly—to the possibility that they may be wrong and others right.

Even when firmly convinced that they are on God's side, mature Christians also recall that God accepts as believers people with imperfect ideologies—in fact, that *all* the people he accepts as believers have imperfect ideologies. They do not treat their political adversaries as enemies, but as colleagues who have a different conception of the good society and who may share many of the same goals even though they differ as to which policy initiatives will get us there.

Christian politics should be defined, first and foremost, not by

154

a set of policy stances but by the virtues such as servanthood, honesty, mutual respect and humility that should characterize any Christian's public involvement. None of these virtues are the exclusive property of believers, but obedient Christians generally should exhibit them in greater depth, particularly as they recognize more clearly than others that all temporal policy debates pale in importance when compared to our eternal destination. I do not wish to minimize the importance of the policy debates in which America is now engaged, but I believe effective Christians in politics will be distinguished more by their means than by their ends—by how they make their points more than by what points they make.

How the Nonreligious Should Integrate Religion and Politics

When I say that Christians (or any other religious believers) should be welcome in the political process, I do not mean to imply that you should feel compelled to agree with their views. I don't even mean to bar detractors of Christian candidates from making religion a campaign issue. As I have stated before, a negative campaign, if waged honestly, is perfectly appropriate speech, and it's the target's job to respond to the charges.

Rather, my objection is to those who would seek categorically to exclude persons of strong religious faith from politics on the grounds that their activity subverts the Constitution's separation of church and state. Excluding such persons is both unjust and greatly undesirable.

It is unjust because religious believers have all the same rights to participate in the public square as anyone else. In separating church from state, our forebears never intended to eliminate religious persons or religiously grounded ideas from public debate; quite the contrary, religious thought played a significant formative role in their own ideas. They wanted only to keep any organized denomination from exerting direct control in the govern-

155

ment. The separation of church from state was designed to protect all churches' autonomy and freedom of worship, not to bar church members from helping to run the state.

Secularists have teamed with Americans fearful of religious squabbles to exclude traditional religious practice from our public places and even virtually to eliminate discussion of religion from our public schools. They have made this arrangement seem fair by illogically equating silence about religion with neutrality toward religion. But to put our youth through twelve years of education, which purports to prepare them for life, without reference to religion is not neutrality at all; it is an unmistakable statement of hostility toward religion, a statement that one can live a complete life without spiritual faith of any sort. Any public institution that sends this message is not neutral toward religion, but systematically discriminating against it.

I do not advocate religious indoctrination or organized school prayer as remedies to this injustice, though I do support a greater role for teaching *about* religion in public school curricula. I simply want to see freedom of individual religious expression restored throughout our society. If we permit even the Ku Klux Klan to erect crosses and hold marches on public property, we should certainly let a schoolteacher keep a Bible on his or her desk.

The absurdity of any effort to exclude religion from public life becomes apparent when one considers that such a step would affect liberal Jews and African-American Christians, not just fundamentalists. Many of black America's civic leaders, in fact, are ordained Christian ministers, and the Revs. Jesse Jackson and Martin Luther King have referred to their Christian foundations as openly as the Rev. Pat Robertson. As our society has wandered toward moral relativism and permissiveness, however, the more distinctly evangelical vision typified by Robertson, which unabashedly asserts that there is no way to salvation or righteousness other than God's way, has proved to be most politically

156

incorrect and has therefore provoked the most strenuous efforts to defeat it. Again, people should be free to criticize such views, just as I in this chapter have faulted conservative Christians for failing to articulate a vision of cultural renewal in a form relevant to non-Christians. But to declare religious voices in the public square subversive is patently unjust.

Not Only Unjust, But Undesirable

An ex-gang member was presenting a seminar to teachers and civic leaders at a local high school. "Once a kid gets into a gang," he explained, "there are only four ways he gets out. He either dies, or goes to jail, or gets a job, or"—he observed matter-of-factly—"he finds Jesus Christ."

The speaker did not belabor the point, nor did he need to. He had provided a vivid reminder of the positive impact spiritual transformation can bring in the lives of youths whom no other program can reach. Why should we *want* to exclude the messengers of such transformation from public life?

I shudder at the prevalence of public schools and grant programs that permit religious organizations to participate only if they promise not to speak of their faith. Not only does this requirement keep some of our most selfless, generous citizens out of the places where they are most needed, but it perpetuates our inability to instill a sense of moral responsibility in our young people. We have spoken to them of no values beyond this material world, and then we wonder why they see no moral evil in committing murder over a pair of sneakers.

Christians should be welcomed in public life not only as purveyors of the moral absolutes our society so desperately needs to recover, but also as generous providers of all kinds of services our government cannot afford to pay for. Whatever their political foibles, conservative Christians play a role disproportionate to their numbers in delivering education, health care, food and shelter to persons in greatest need. They care for prisoners, take unwanted children into their homes, and start recreation programs in inner cities, solely out of their love for people. If we push them into cultural isolation or discourage them from public service, our whole society will suffer.

Christians are also well suited to help all of us keep politics in perspective. Since the Great Society years of the 1960s, our nation has tended to forget the limits of politics, trying to solve our problems through social engineering. Those without a strong religious commitment can be expected to place greater confidence in political solutions, because they have nothing higher in which to place their faith. Christians should lead the way in pointing out that our deepest needs, socially as well as spiritually, cannot ultimately be addressed through politics, and that to pretend that they can only sets the stage for ultimate disillusionment.

Admittedly, many Christians have themselves come slowly to this discovery over the last two decades. At first they seemed to believe that electing the right president would turn the nation around. When that did not suffice, they intensified their efforts to elect more of their favored politicians at all levels of government. While not abandoning that pursuit, many of them are perceiving that cultural renewal hinges upon touching hearts and shaping values and that lasting political change in a democratic republic can only follow, not precede, a multitude of individual, internal transformations.

Don Eberly, in *Restoring the Good Society,* and former Secretary of Education William Bennett, through his *Book of Virtues, Index of Leading Cultural Indicators* and countless public speeches, have led the way in contending that American society needs to relearn, more than anything else, how to cultivate virtue. They have also argued persuasively that we cannot hope to achieve this goal if religion, historically the primary teacher of virtue, is continually pushed to the margins of American public life. Whatever else one thinks of the Judeo-Christian tradition, there should be no doubt that persons who take its teachings on eternal judgment seriously will not succumb, like so many politicians, to the temptations of personal glory or material gain.

Now Let's Join Hands

This chapter has attempted to build a philosophical foundation on which religious and nonreligious persons, whether they agree or disagree on matters of policy, should be able to grant the legitimacy of each other's presence in public life and treat each other with respect rather than innuendo. Let's summarize by giving several practical pointers on how to handle religion-and-politics issues honestly and fairly.

1. Begin by recognizing that, in the political sector, the shared interests of religious and nonreligious persons far outweigh their differences and provide ample basis for cooperation.

2. Identify the societal values that religion has supported and encourage these (and religion's role in inculcating them) in nonsectarian but nonsecularist terms.

3. You can use religious arguments to support your public policies when in church, but when in public (i.e., not explicitly religious) settings, stick to nonreligious arguments. If you don't have sufficient nonreligious arguments to support your position, quit advocating it as public policy.

4. Pursue *fairness*, not *neutrality*, toward religion. Neutrality, in an attempt not to favor one faith over another, too often silences religion completely. Fairness, while not preferring one religion over another in the civil sphere, lets all legitimate religious voices be heard. (As a practical application, your public high school's humanities class should be permitted to invite representatives of all locally represented religious groups to visit and discuss their belief systems, rather than being prohibited from inviting any of them.)

159

5. Don't impose your religious position on your political party or organization. You can be personally a vocal Christian, but unless you know that nobody in the organization will object, the group's prayers and statements should be nonsectarian.

6. Recognize nonsectarian acknowledgments of a Creator as appropriate in the civil sphere.

7. Judge candidates by their stances and their integrity, not by their religious orientation. It is perfectly appropriate to inquire about candidates' faith commitments, as a means of probing their character and core values, but outward religious profession, personal integrity and political competence do not always go together. Accordingly, don't ask a candidate "Are you born again?" in a public forum, as if this were an essential qualification for office.

8. Remember that religion, like politics, is a sensitive issue to many persons, and that you dishonor your own position if you fail to handle religious or political disagreements with civility and respectfulness.

9. Finally, never reduce religion to its worldly benefits. True religion has practical usefulness (e.g., in teaching moral responsibility and respect for law), but its primary and ultimate value lies in its unique ability to make people right with God.

10

ARE YOU
READY
TO PLAY?

. . . .

Well, you've completed the introductory course. If I knew you wanted to read another hundred pages, I could go on to discuss policy issues, coalition-building, speaking styles and many other topics. But a book for the average reader should be short and sweet. If this book has whetted your appetite for more political training, your favorite party or interest group should be amply equipped to provide it.

My goal in writing this book has not been to enthrall you about politics, though I hope you might find it a bit more appetizing now. Nor has it been to motivate you to some minimum level of political activity others might consider every citizen's duty. Once when teaching a seminar on politics I was asked what I felt should be the minimum level of political involvement for a citizen. I surprised the group with my answer: zero. Politics is not everything, and it has no claim to preeminence among the various sectors of human activity. It is one way to address human needs, but there are many others. I have no problem with the person who says he or she is called to serve family, church, Little League and coworkers and has no time left to do politics.

Whether you've fallen in love with politics or not, I hope I have achieved two more modest goals: to make the world of politics more accessible to you, and to urge you to cultivate a spirit of servanthood in any political activity you do undertake. At the very least, I fancy that perhaps, by instilling a greater appreciation and sense of shared ownership of our system of government, I have increased your motivation to pay your taxes. Whether you go beyond that to any further political involvement is up to you. If you do, though, I hope you will steer clear of the desperation and ravenous ambition that drive so many political operatives.

On this note, my last real-life story recalls not a smashing political victory but an unlikely good deed.

One day the director of a technical school phoned me to plead on behalf of a model student. Abigail, a single parent of three young children, was attending his school with the help of a publicly funded job-training initiative. During the summer, she and her children had moved out of public housing into a nearby apartment. But not until she sought to enroll the two older children in kindergarten and first grade for the new school year did she discover that the move placed them in territory belonging to a different elementary school.

This change destroyed the intricate schedule Abigail and her child-care provider had worked out. The children were not on a bus schedule because their apartment was too close to their new school, but the child-care provider, who was within walking distance of the old school, had no way to transport the children to the new school.

162

The school district's administrator was singularly unhelpful, other than to inform Abigail that the children could not remain in their former school because a citywide desegregation plan permitted no exceptions. Running out of options and tearful at the prospect of dropping out of her training program, Abigail alerted her school director, who brought me into the discussion.

In investigating the situation I confirmed that Abigail's children definitely could not stay in their original school. But I also discovered that they might qualify for busing on the basis that, regardless of where their home was located, they would be traveling to school from a location outside walking distance. While I pursued this option the children missed the first day of school and would have missed the second—had it not occurred to me that I could drive them to school.

It was an unusual form of constituent service, but both the child-care site and the school were within two miles of our office. So, after visiting with the children the previous evening to help them feel comfortable with me, I made three quick round trips that day—taking Heather to first grade in the morning, Robin to kindergarten at noon, and returning both of them to child care after school. We had a wonderful time, and by that evening the children were placed on a bus schedule starting the next day.

On my way back to the office after dropping Heather at school, I broke down and cried. Not because a caring mother had had to pass on to me the special experience of introducing her children to their new school, though I did feel bad about that. I cried over the injustice that churches, social workers and other service providers carry out such acts of love every day and receive so little recognition, while politicians often engaged more in posturing and grandstanding than in meaningful service get so much undeserved praise.

I take heart in the knowledge that the praise faithful servants receive from God will outlast fleeting acclaim from men and women anyhow. But I also yearn to see politics become a field more populated by honest servants and a less fertile ground for ambitious, smooth-tongued but uncaring deceivers. The only way to make the fakers unwelcome is to have more honest politicians actively involved, knowing the game, exposing the less honorable players. If you're ready to play by those rules—and to help make government and politics exist *for* the people—welcome aboard.

Further Resources

Suggested Reading

Barone, Michael, and Grant Ujifusa. *The Almanac of American Politics*. Washington, D.C.: National Journal. Valuable resource (updated yearly) on the basic facts of American politics at the state and national levels.

Carter, Stephen L. *The Culture of Disbelief: How American Law and Politics Trivialize Religious Devotion*. New York: Basic Books, 1993. Widely acclaimed reanalysis of the place of religion in American public life, particularly influential because it did *not* emerge from the Christian Right.

Eberly, Don E. *Restoring the Good Society: A New Vision for Politics and Culture*. Grand Rapids, Mich.: Baker, 1994. An excellent essay on recovering civic and moral responsibility in America. Includes useful discussions of the relationship between religion and politics and of the role—and limits—of politics in restoring the culture.

Hatfield, Mark. *Not Quite So Simple*. New York: Harper & Row, 1968. Thought-provoking reflections by a U.S. senator of evangelical faith who vigorously opposed the Vietnam War and who has gone on to make his mark in the Senate as a reflective, atypical Republican.

Hunter, James Davison. *Culture Wars: The Struggle to Define America*. New York: Basic Books, 1991. One of the nation's most prominent academic sociologists analyzes the cultural battles that have dominated contemporary American politics.

Jackley, John L. *Hill Rat: Blowing the Lid Off Congress*. Washington, D.C.: Regnery Gateway, 1992. A former Capitol Hill staffer exposes the seamy side of congressional politics.

McGrath, Dennis J., and Dane Smith. *Professor Wellstone Goes to Washington: The*

Inside Story of a Grassroots U.S. Senate Campaign. Minneapolis: U. of Minnesota Press, 1995. A fast-paced story told by two newspaper reporters who covered the heated 1992 race in which Democrat Paul Wellstone unseated Rudy Boschwitz. Particularly valuable because the reporters were privy to the inside workings of each campaign and because Wellstone's was indeed a grassroots effort.

O'Neill, Tip, with William Novak. *Man of the House: The Life and Political Memoirs of Speaker Tip O'Neill.* New York: Random House, 1987.

O'Neill, Tip, with Gary Hymel. *All Politics Is Local, and Other Rules of the Game.* New York: Times Books, 1994. These two books are full of wonderful stories and invaluable insights from a consummate politician who rose to become Speaker of the U.S. House.

Price, David F. *The Congressional Experience: A View from the Hill.* Boulder, Colo.: Westview, 1992. Both academic and practical insights from a Duke political-science professor who was, at the time of publication, in his third term as a congressman.

Reed, Ralph E. *Politically Incorrect: What Religious Conservatives Really Think.* Waco, Tex.: Word, 1994. A thorough political statement by the highly sophisticated executive director of the Christian Coalition.

Skillen, James W. *The Scattered Voice: Christians at Odds in the Public Square.* Grand Rapids, Mich.: Zondervan, 1990. Balanced presentation and critique of a variety of Christian political views.

Getting Local Information

Often people shy away from political activity because they don't know basic information, such as who their legislators are or when those legislators will be up for election again, and they are embarrassed to admit their ignorance. My advice is simple: don't be embarrassed. Your nearest public library or League of Women Voters chapter should be able to direct you to the information you need, and within half an hour you'll be better equipped than most Americans.

In my county the League of Women Voters publishes brochures listing local officeholders. In addition, a local utility company produces, as a public service, multicolor maps that show the boundaries of each state and federal legislative district, along with the name, address and phone number of each legislator. Your librarian or your municipal office can probably help you find similar sources of information in your community. You may also wish to contact a local office of the Democratic or Republican party or your county's board of elections for assistance.

Citizen Organizations

Following is a sampling of national organizations committed to informing citizens and soliciting their involvement with various political issues. This sample covers the political spectrum but is *not* intended to be exhaustive. If this list does not include an organization promoting the issue in which you are most interested, you may wish to consult *Washington Representatives* (1995 edition ed. Arthur C. Close, J. Valerie Steele and Michael E. Buckner; Washington, D.C.: Columbia Books), which provides a listing of all the organizations represented around Capitol Hill and from which the brief descriptions provided here are drawn.

Christian Coalition, P.O. Box 1990, Chesapeake, VA 23320. (804) 424-2630. The preeminent grassroots organization for conservative-leaning Christians since its founding by Pat Robertson in 1989.

Citizen Action, 1730 Rhode Island Ave. NW, Suite 403, Washington, DC 20036. (202) 775-1580. Liberal-leaning group active on domestic issues such as health care, campaign finance and the environment.

Common Cause, 2030 M St. NW, Washington, DC 20036. (202) 833-1200. A "citizens' lobby" primarily concerned for honest and accountable government, best known for its prominence on issues of government ethics, campaign finance and the role of political-action committees.

League of Conservation Voters, 1707 L St. NW, Suite 750, Washington, DC 20036. (202) 785-8683. The political arm of the environmental movement, it rates members of Congress according to their stands on energy and environmental issues.

National Federation of Independent Business, 600 Maryland Ave. SW, Suite 700, Washington, DC 20024. (202) 554-9000. This voice of small business gained prominence by coordinating much of the opposition to President Clinton's health-care reform proposal.

National Rifle Association, 11250 Waples Mill Rd., Fairfax, VA 22030. (703) 267-1000. The primary political voice of gun owners and sportsmen, the NRA has long been considered a master of political muscle by friends and foes alike.

National Right to Life Committee, 419 Seventh St. NW, Suite 500, Washington, DC 20004. (202) 626-8820. The primary political arm of the prolife movement.

National Taxpayers Union, 713 Maryland Ave. NE, Washington, DC 20002. (202) 543-1300. The NTU promotes tax cuts, smaller government and balanced budgets. It rates members of Congress according to their records on government spending.

People for the American Way, 2000 M St. NW, Suite 400, Washington, DC 20036. (202) 467-4999. Founded in response to the Christian Right, it is most active in areas of church-state separation, religious liberty and free expression.

Public Citizen, 2000 P St. NW, Washington, DC 20036. (202) 833-3000. Founded by Ralph Nader, this organization advocates for consumer rights, product and workplace safety, and government accountability.

United We Stand America, P.O. Box 516087, Dallas, TX 75251. (214) 960-9100. The grassroots organization formed by Ross Perot for his 1992 presidential campaign, and which Perot hopes will become the basis of a third political party.